MEAD

Making, Exhibiting and Judging

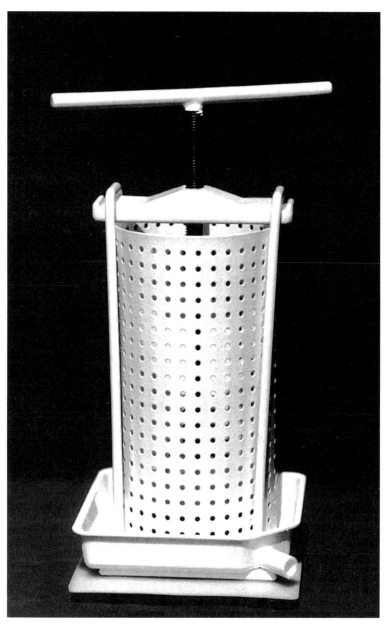

Fruit press

MEAD
Making, Exhibiting & Judging

Harry R.C. Riches, M.D., F.R.C.P.
Past President, British Beekeepers Association

BEE BOOKS NEW & OLD
10 Quay Road, Charlestown,
Cornwall

ISBN 0 905652 41 X

Books by Harry Riches still available

Honey Marketing ISBN 0 905652 41 X
Published by BBNO, 1989

A Handbook of Beekeeping ISBN 0907908 62 4
Published by NBB, 1992

Printed in Great Britain by
BPC Wheatons Ltd.
Exeter

CONTENTS

LIST OF ILLUSTRATIONS

PREFACE

A number of books have been written about mead, but sadly, most are now out of print and not easily available. For that reason it is hoped that this new small book will be a useful source of up to date information for those who wish to make this unique beverage.

I have endeavoured to write a simple introductory guide to making, exhibiting and judging mead based on my personal experience which extends over more than twenty five years. I have not attempted to review all the various methods which have been advocated in earlier literature because I felt that might confuse the beginner and make the subject appear too difficult.

My qualifications for writing this book are twofold. First, in a quarter of a century of mead and wine making I have made every possible mistake so I can claim familiarity with all the problems! Second, despite those difficulties, I have enjoyed success on the show bench at all levels. My initial first prize for mead at the National Honey Show was in 1973 and I have received many awards since. I was particularly proud to win the House of Lords wine goblet awarded for mead at the National Honey Show Golden Jubilee in 1981. In recent years, with some regret, I have curtailed exhibiting because of numerous judging engagements at major shows, including the National Honey Show in London.

Although I believe that my ideas and methods are largely conventional and not controversial, I hope, nevertheless, that they are of interest.

Finally, I wish to thank John Kinross of Bee Books New & Old for encouraging me to put pen to paper. I hope he doesn't regret it!

Harry Riches.
Northwood, Middlesex.

INTRODUCTION

Mead is an alcoholic beverage made by the fermentation of honey in water by yeast. It was possibly the first alcoholic drink that man imbibed but clear proof of that is lacking. Obviously, because honey was the earliest available sweetening agent containing fermentable sugars, it is easy to imagine that by accident or experimentation, primitive man discovered that honeycomb left in water produced a pleasant drinkable fluid with cheering effects! That, of course, is pure speculation. On firmer ground, archaeologists claim there is evidence that some sort of wine was drunk 10,000 to 12,000 years ago. Very recently, in 1996, a jar discovered at a Stone Age site in Iran, and dating from 5,400 to 5,000 BC, was found to contain traces of wine residues. The earliest *documentary* evidence suggests that a fermented honey beverage was drunk in India some 4000 years ago.

The early Greeks and Romans drank mead but it appears that they consumed larger quantities of grape wine. It is well documented that the Romans imported much wine for their occupying garrisons in the British Isles and also planted vineyards here in the 3rd century. In the colder parts of Northern Europe, however, mead and grain beers were more widely available and remained the popular alcoholic drink after the withdrawal of the Roman legions.

Much early mead was low in alcohol content and more in the nature of beer than wine. Perhaps because of poor quality, due to ignorance of the fermentation process, unpleasant off-flavours were common and to mask these, herbs were added, thus making metheglin rather than plain mead. Queen Elizabeth I is reputed to have been a regular drinker of metheglin.

A few vineyards persisted in Britain after the Roman evacuation, usually associated with the monasteries. At the time of the Norman conquest there were 38 listed in the Domesday Book. It is reasonable to assume that the French brought with them their established drinking habits and grape wine became increasingly available. Imports later rocketed when Henry II married Queen Eleanor of Aquitaine whose possessions included Bordeaux. It is said that more than a 1000 ships were engaged in the cross-channel wine trade at that time. The imports of cheap French wine precipitated the demise of British vineyards and their elimination was completed when Henry VIII acted against the monasteries.

Beer and imported cheap wine became the drink of the masses whilst mead, and its variations, still found favour in rural beekeeping communities. The Industrial Revolution saw a great movement of population into the towns where beer and gin were the popular drinks. Gradually much of the rural skill of home wine and mead making was lost but in a small way beekeepers continued the craft. Although home wine making was never restricted by law, so long as the product was not sold, home beer making was discouraged when Mr Gladstone introduced legislation in the 1880 Inland Revenue Act which made it a requirement to have a licence to brew beer. It was not until 1963 that Mr Reginald Maudling, a Conservative chancellor, proposed that this part of the Act should be repealed. This laudable action was followed by a resurgence of interest in home brewing and wine making. For about 25 years, shops selling wine and brewing equipment and ingredients flourished, wine guilds and clubs were formed and wine shows and competitions arranged. By 1984, when this 'cottage industry' peaked, it was estimated that 12.5% of the UK population were making wine or beer at home. Sadly, interest has declined in recent years but enthusiasm for mead still persists amongst a minority of beekeepers. I sincerely hope that this will continue and that many more will be encouraged to make and enjoy what is undoubtedly a unique beverage. Furthermore, apart from deriving pleasure and satisfaction from making something nice to drink, they should also be proud to be the privileged custodians of a skill of great antiquity.

CHAPTER 1

INGREDIENTS

Mead has been defined as an alcoholic beverage which results from the fermentation of honey in water by yeast. Although by definition the basic ingredients are honey, water and yeast, there are other important supplementary ingredients necessary for making a good product. Together with the primary constituents, these will be considered in a little detail.

Honey

Nectar is a sugary liquid which flowers secrete in order to attract insects. It is the starting substance from which honey is made. Whilst collecting this food, the hairy bodies of bees become dusted with pollen which is thereby transported from one flower to another. By offering an attractant to insects, plants achieve wide dispersal of their pollen with the consequent benefits of cross fertilisation. Nectar is not the only attractant, however, because pollen, which is rich in proteins, is essential nourishment for their young brood and is collected in large quantity.

Nectar is essentially a dilute water solution of sugars together with traces of proteins, salts, vitamins, and aromatic substances, the precise composition varying with the plant species from which it was derived. It is produced by small glandular organs called nectaries which in an open flowers such as apple, are located at the base of the petals. Nectaries can, however, be located in other positions within a flower depending on the species, and in some plants are found outside the flower on stems and leaves.

The predominant sugar in most nectars is sucrose, the same sugar which is in everyday use on our tables for sweetening. Since 70% to 80% of nectar is water, the concentration of sugars is low, and as only tiny quantities of nectar are secreted by each flower, bees have to do a prodigious amount of work to produce a pound (0.54 kg) of honey. It has been calculated that a bee may visit more than a thousand flowers to fill its honey crop with between 40 and 70 mg of nectar, from which no more than 20 mg of honey will be produced. Based on such figures it has been estimated that to produce one pound (0.54 kg) of honey the bee/miles flown might equal three orbits of the earth!

As nectar is collected from flowers it is diluted with bee saliva. This contains enzymes, the main one being invertase which breaks down sucrose into the two simpler sugars, glucose and fructose. These chemical changes to nectar begin in the honey crop of the foraging bee and is continued in the hive where the nectar is processed further by 'house' bees. By prolonged manipulation in their mouth-parts, aided by the warmth of the hive, the chemical changes are completed and water evaporated so that nectar is slowly transformed into honey. When the water content is reduced below 20% it is sealed in the combs. At this stage, a high quality floral honey, should contain constituents in approximately the following proportions: glucose 31.3%, fructose 38.2%, sucrose 1.3%, maltose 7.3%, higher sugars 1.5%, total acid 0.5%, ash 0.169% nitrogen 0.041%, and water 17.2%.

Nectar is the origin of the vast majority of all honey produced in Great Britain. However, bees will collect the sweet sticky substance known as honeydew which is excreted by certain plant-sucking insects, such as aphids, which are found at times in large numbers on plants and trees. Honeydew produces a dark coloured honey of strong flavour which is not suitable for making good mead.

The aroma, taste and colour of honey varies with the plant species from which nectar was gathered. White clover, oil seed rape, willow herb, for example, give a light coloured honey, whilst blackberry, apple, dandelion produce a medium colour, and honeydew and heather honey are typically dark.

As a general rule, high quality mead is best made from a light or medium coloured floral honey which has a mild delicate aroma and flavour. Strongly flavoured dark honey should be reserved for sweet mead.

Water

Some mead makers advise the use of distilled water or filtered rain water. I am not convinced that this is a significant benefit and have always used good quality unfiltered domestic drinking water.

Yeast

Yeasts are unicellular fungi which are very widely distributed. A container of dilute sugar solution open to the atmosphere will, in a few days, start to ferment because of contamination by airborne wild yeast. Unfortunately, these wild yeasts are not suitable for brewing quality wines because they frequently produce off flavours, are quickly inhibited by rising alcohol content, and do not tolerate low concentrations of sulphur dioxide. To make good mead it is necessary to use an authentic wine yeast of the *Saccharomyces cerivisiae* strain. A number of varieties are commercially available from suppliers of home wine making items. For a dry mead a 'Chablis' yeast would be appropriate and for a sweet mead 'Sauterne' or 'Tokay' would be the choice.

Yeast can be purchased in dry or liquid form. Dry is convenient but is best brought to life in a 'starter bottle' before use. The latter is simply a small clean bottle, sterilised in boiling water, cooled, and to which is then added about quarter of a pint of clean water which has been boiled and cooled. To the bottle is then added a teaspoon of sugar, a teaspoon of lemon juice or a pinch of citric acid, and a quarter of a spoon of Marmite. Mix well, add the dry yeast, place a bung of cotton wool in the neck of the bottle and stand in a warm room or airing cupboard. Within 48 hours the solution in the bottle will become cloudy and bubbles will be seen around the surface edge. This indicates that the yeast is alive and ready for use.

Essential additives

(a) *Acid*

Wine yeast will only grow well in an acid medium. Although honey is slightly acid it does not provide sufficient acidity when dissolved in water to give good yeast growth. Fermentation will, therefore, be impaired. Correct acidity also discourages growth of contaminating unwanted bacteria. Furthermore, a good drinkable mead requires a balanced acidity to give a fresh clean effect in the mouth. For these various reasons acid has to be added to the brew, or 'must' as it is called by professional brewers and wine makers.

A simple way to add acid is to squeeze the juice from a good sized lemon and add this to a gallon of must. Alternatively, add two level teaspoons of citric acid and one level teaspoon of tartaric acid to each gallon. In weight aim to add 10 to 15 grams of acid per gallon.

Acidity testing strip paper (similar to litmus paper) can be obtained which when dipped into the must indicates acidity by a colour change which can be read against a scale. On the scientific pH scale the acidity of the must should be around 3.2 to 3.4, perhaps a little less (i.e. more acid) if a sweet mead is intended.

(b) *Yeast nutrient*

Rapidly growing yeast needs nitrogen to build its cell proteins. Honey is deficient in nitrogen containing substances so nutrient salts in the form of ammonium sulphate and phosphate should be added to the must. Yeast nutrient preparations containing these salts can be obtained from any wine makers shop and should be used according to the specific instructions.

(c) *Tannin*

An important ingredient of grapes and other wine making fruit which honey lacks, is tannin. Without tannin to give some astringency a wine tastes flat and insipid without 'bite'. Strong tea which has stood in the pot until cold, contains tannin and has been used by mead makers, about two tablespoons to the gallon of must. Tannin preparations, either liquid or dry, can be purchased. Dry grape tannin is preferred by the writer, a quarter teaspoon to the gallon of must.

(d) *Vitamins*

It has been shown that Vitamin B_1 helps yeast to thrive and to this end one 3mg tablet per gallon can be added to the must.

Vitamin C (ascorbic acid) is a potent anti-oxidant. A crushed 200mg tablet should be added to the must if chemical acids are used but will not be necessary if raw lemon juice is used as the acid source. Exposure of wine and mead to air causes it to become oxidised, a deterioration which shows itself as a browning of white wines and a flabby Madeira-like off flavour. Vitamin C is a helpful preventative of this but is not a complete safeguard and careful wine making technique is essential. (See later)

CHAPTER 2

EQUIPMENT

Only a few essential items of equipment are necessary in order to start making mead. They are fortunately cheap and readily available from any shop supplying wine making items.

Requirements
Food-grade plastic bucket or fermentation bin
1 gallon glass demijohn
Air lock and bung for the demijohn
About 4 feet of plastic tubing for siphoning
Large plastic funnel
Bottle cleaning brush
Wine bottles and corks

It should always be remembered that wine making equipment must be kept scrupulously clean, not just visibly clean, but devoid of all those bacteria and fungi which are everywhere in the atmosphere and ready to contaminate. This means that equipment has to be *sterilized.* This is easily achieved by the use of Campden tablets containing metabisulphite which, when dissolved in water containing a little citric acid, liberate sulphur dioxide, a potent sterilizing agent. Four Campden tablets dissolved in a pint of previously boiled and cooled water to which a pinch of citric acid is added makes a very effective sterilizing fluid for rinsing the inside of demijohns, bottles, siphon tubing etc.

For cleaning and sterilizing larger items such as fermentation bins, buckets, etc. 'Chempro SDP' is very effective. This is a commercial product which sterilizes by the liberation of chlorine. It is available at wine makers shops.

Throughout many years of making mead I have found a

hydrometer to be an invaluable piece of equipment. Although it is possible to make mead without one, in my view it is an essential item.

Without getting too technical, a hydrometer is a simple instrument which measures the specific gravity of a fluid; specific gravity being the ratio of the density of a substance to the density of water. Those used by wine makers are shaped like a coarse fishing float. When placed in a jar of water the hydrometer will stabilize and float in a position when the weight of water displaced equals the weight of the instrument. This point is marked as 1.000 on the instrument, the specific gravity of water. A sugar solution is heavier than water and because of this the float (hydrometer) will not displace so much of that solution as it would in pure water and will not, therefore, sink so far. On the other hand, alcohol being lighter than water, in a mixture of alcohol and water with no sugar present, the hydrometer will sink more.

The hydrometer is marked with a scale which indicates the Specific Gravity of the fluid under test and by reference to tables the sugar content of that fluid can be deduced. (See below)

Knowledge of the sugar content of a must before fermentation is important and, in addition, it is helpful to check that it is falling during fermentation and at what point fermentation ceases.

A simple plastic hydrometer is very cheap and a most worthwhile investment.

GRAVITY TABLE

Specific Gravity	Sugar per gallon (oz/gallon)	Potential alcohol (%/volume)
1.000	0	0
1.010	2	0.9
1.015	4	1.6
1.020	7	2.3
1.025	9	3
1.030	12	3.7
1.035	15	4.4
1.040	17	5
1.045	19	5.8
1.050	21	6.5
1.055	23	7.2
1.060	25	7.8
1.065	27	8.6
1.070	29	9.2
1.075	31	9.9
1.080	33	10.6
1.085	36	11.3
1.090	38	12
1.095	40	12.7
1.100	42	13.4
1.105	44	14.1
1.110	46	14.9

Note. The above table refers to *sugar* per gallon. The mead maker must bear in mind that honey contains only about 80% fermentable sugar and allowance must be made. Very roughly, 1lb of sugar is equivalent to 1.25 lb of honey.

CHAPTER 3

FERMENTATION

Fermentation is the name given to the activity of yeast in converting sugar into ethyl alcohol and carbon dioxide. It was the great French chemist and bacteriologist, Louis Pasteur (1822-95), who first elucidated that fermentation was caused by yeasts. We now know that the actual agent produced by yeast to bring about the chemical changes of fermentation is the enzyme zymase. It must be emphasized that the breakdown of sugar into carbon dioxide and ethyl alcohol by yeast only occurs in anaerobic conditions, i.e. with the exclusion of air. If air is freely available to yeast the chemical changes will progress further so that the end products are water and carbon dioxide and no alcohol.

These changes can be represented by the following chemical equations.

In anaerobic conditions

$$C_6H_{12}O_6 \xrightarrow{\text{yeast}} 2C_2H_5OH + 2CO_2$$

In aerobic conditions

$$C_6H_{12}O_6 + 6O_2 \xrightarrow{\text{yeast}} 6CO_2 + 6H_2O$$

To produce an alcoholic beverage it is therefore essential that fermentation occurs in anaerobic conditions. This is achieved very simply by the use of an air-lock in the top of the demijohn. However, air should not be excluded immediately yeast is added to the must because the presence of air initially helps the yeast to grow quickly. The common practice, therefore, is to prepare the must in a sterile bucket, add the yeast, cover with a cloth and keep in a warm environment for 48 hours, stirring occasionally, before putting into a demijohn with an air-lock in place to produce anaerobic conditions.

As indicated in the previous chapter, only genuine wine yeasts should be used.

The temperature at which fermentation occurs is important. If conditions are too warm fermentation will become very vigorous causing frothing and possible over-flow from the jar. This excessive turbulent activity also causes aromatic volatile substances to be lost which is undesirable. A steady cool fermentation is best but the temperature must not be too cold otherwise fermentation will stop.

When the must is prepared in a bucket and the yeast added a temperature of about 70°F (20°C) is appropriate, but after transfer to a demijohn cooler conditions are desirable, say 60°F (15°C). Careful control of temperature is necessary because significant heat is liberated by the fermentation process and an excessive rise in temperature will kill the yeast.

Yeast thrives best in the dark so the demijohn should, ideally, be placed in a cupboard or somewhere similar away from bright light.

The fermentation which has been described above is the fundamental process of wine making and is often referred to as the primary fermentation. However, another fermentation may occur, especially in wines incorporating fruit juices and is known as the malolactic fermentation. This usually occurs some time after the completion of the primary process and is often called the secondary fermentation. It is caused by micro-organisms, Lactic bacteria, which break down malic acid into lactic acid. The latter is less acidic and gives the wine a smoother less harsh acidity. A malolactic fermentation can be considered desirable but will only occur in plain mead when malic acid is used as the acid additive. It is a common happening in fruit meads such as melomels, cyser, hippocras etc.

The chemical equation for the malolactic fermentation can be written as follows

$$COOH\text{-}CHOH\text{-}CH_2\text{-}COOH \longrightarrow COOH\text{-}CHOH\text{-}CH_3 + CO_2$$

            malic acid   lactic acid   carbon dioxide

As carbon dioxide is liberated in the reaction, the recurrence of bubbling in a demijohn or bottle after a period of quiescence is strongly suggestive that a malolactic fermentation is occurring.

CHAPTER 4

METHOD OF MAKING MEAD

Mead can be made dry or sweet, the only difference being that in dry mead all the fermentable sugars contained in the must have been completely used by the yeast so that no sweetness remains, whereas in a sweet mead some residual unfermented sugar gives the beverage a sweet taste. A simple basic method for making dry mead is as follows.

Recipe

3 lbs of light honey

6 pints of water

1 teaspoon of yeast nutrient

$1/4$ teaspoon of grape tannin (or 2 tablespoons of cold strong tea)

Juice of a lemon

Tab Vitamin B_1

Chablis yeast

Raw honey contains many wild yeasts and fungi which will grow and ferment, if allowed to do so, when honey is mixed with water. This is undesirable and should be prevented because the fermentation they cause can produce unpleasant off-flavours and aromas. Furthermore, these wild yeasts are incapable of producing the necessary concentration of alcohol for a good wine and are intolerant of even very low concentrations of sulphur dioxide. This latter characteristic is an important deficiency because there are circumstances when it is desirable to add low concentrations of sulphur dioxide to the brew in the form of Campden tablets, to prevent bacterial contamination, without running the risk of killing the yeast.

The honey and water mixture (known as the 'must') should therefore be sterilized before an authentic wine yeast is added.

There are two widely used methods, one uses heat and the other metabisulphite (Campden tablets). For a small volume of must, such as a single gallon, heat sterilization is easy but for larger volumes a cold procedure is more convenient

Heat sterilization of must

Place the six pints of water in a large saucepan, add the honey, stir until dissolved, and add the yeast nutrient, crushed Vitamin B₁ tablet, lemon juice and tannin. Heat to 150°F (66°C) and simmer at this temperature for a few minutes only, skim off the froth, cover with a clean cloth and allow to cool.

When the temperature has fallen to 70°F (21°C) pour into a clean sterile fermentation bin or bucket and add the wine yeast which has been activated in a starter bottle as described in the previous chapter. Cover with a clean cloth and place in a warm cupboard. If tested with a hydrometer the specific gravity of the must at this stage will probably be around 1.100.

Within 24 hours bubbles and froth on the surface will indicate an active fermentation. After a further 24 hours the fermenting must should be poured into a clean sterile demijohn and an air-lock fitted. The fluid in the air-lock which makes the seal can be either water containing a little metabisulphite or glycerine. The latter has the advantage that it does not evaporate away so quickly.

In the initial period the fermentation will be vigorous with the generation of some heat and it is for this reason that it is best to place the demijohn somewhere in the dark at a temperature of about 60°F (15°C). During this early phase the must should not fill the demijohn completely because a very active fermentation may cause it to overflow. It is wise to leave a space of a few inches in the top of the demijohn until the vigorous fermentation has settled and then top up with water to within an inch of the bung holding the air-lock.

The demijohn should be left in a cool place until fermentation is complete as indicated by the cessation of bubbles escaping through the air-lock. This may take four to six weeks by which time the mead will begin to clear and a deposit will collect in the bottom of the jar. The mead should then be siphoned off the deposit into a clean sterile container. Wine makers call this siphoning procedure 'racking'. After discarding the deposit (the 'lees') the demijohn should be rinsed clean and refilled with the mead. One Campden tablet should be added and the jar topped up with water. At this stage the mead should taste dry and the specific gravity should be approaching 1.000. When fully fermented to bone dryness the specific gravity will be lower, possibly 0.995.

The mead should be stored in a cool dark place and after a few weeks, if further significant deposit collects in the bottom of the demijohn, it should be racked again. After about a year it should be clear and bright and can be bottled. In a few more months it should be ready to drink. It seems a fact of life that beekeepers who make mead are tempted to drink it too early. In my opinion a dry mead improves if kept for a year or two in cellar conditions and sweet meads benefit by keeping for at least five years. Patience is required!

Sweet mead is started similarly except that it is desirable to add a little more lemon juice, say that from two small lemons, and a Sauterne or Tokay yeast would be preferable.

After the initial fermentation, when the Specific Gravity has fallen below 1.005, a further 4 oz of honey is added and the fermentation allowed to continue. A few weeks later the Specific Gravity is again tested and if below 1.005 a further 4 oz of honey added. This procedure is repeated at intervals (called 'feeding the must') until the build up of alcohol reaches a level which suppresses the yeast activity and fermentation ceases. At this point there remains in the must some unfermented honey which gives the brew its sweetness. A sweet table mead should have a Specific Gravity of something between 1.005 and 1.010 but tastes vary and you should make mead which suits your palate. A heavy strong dessert mead could have a Specific Gravity nearer 1.020.

Clearly, in the process of feeding the must until the yeast is inhibited by alcohol concentration, a further one to two pounds of honey may be added to the original three. The end product will inevitably, therefore, be very strong and many would consider it too potent for a table wine.

To produce sweet table mead which is not too high in alcohol it is necessary to stop the fermentation at a Specific Gravity of about 1.010 when perhaps only about 3 to 3½ lbs of honey are used in the recipe. A common method is to add two Campden tablets to the demijohn and rack after two days, repeating the process after a week or two if fermentation has not stopped completely. The method works on most occasions but is not 100% certain and accidents can occur if fermentation re-starts after bottling. Many wine makers can describe experiences when corks have been blown or bottles exploded ! Another disadvantage is that the high concentration of sulphur dioxide liberated by the heavy use of metabisulphite may take a long time to disperse.

The more certain and easier way to stop fermentation is to use the potassium salt of sorbic acid. The polyhydric alcohol, sorbitol, is found in the fruit of the Mountain Ash (Sorbus aucuparia) and in some other fruits. When absorbed by yeast cells, sorbates block their metabolism of other sugars and the yeast dies. It has no adverse effects on human nutrition and is used quite widely in the food industry. It is available from wine makers shops as 'Sorbistat', sometimes called 'Wine Stabiliser', and should be used as advised on the packet. In tablet form the dose is often one tablet to the gallon.

In practice, the mead should be racked when the Specific Gravity falls to 1.010, a Campden tablet and the sorbate added, and the mead left for a week or so to ensure that fermentation has stopped before bottling.

Cold sterilization of the must

Some wine makers believe that heating a must to sterilize destroys some of the contained aromatic substances. For that reason they prefer a cold sterilizing method. On the other hand, those who prefer heating claim that their method coagulates traces of proteins and colloids which come from pollen in the honey and this results in a clearer brighter end product. The only observation I can make is that I have never had any difficulty in producing clear bright mead with cold sterilizing and it is certainly more convenient when large volumes of must are involved.

The practical method of cold sterilizing is very simple. Dissolve the honey in six pints of water in a bucket or fermentation bin, add the yeast nutrient, lemon juice, tannin and one crushed Campden tablet. Stir, cover with a cloth and place in a warm position. After 48 hours stir vigorously to get rid of some of the sulphur dioxide and to introduce plenty of oxygen into the must. Add the yeast which has been activated in a starter bottle. It is essential in this method to introduce an active yeast because the residual sulphur dioxide would be sufficient to inhibit a dried inactive yeast if that was used. Keep in the covered bin in a warm position until traces of froth begin to appear on the surface of the must indicating that fermentation has started. This may take a day or two because initial yeast growth is slowed by the residual sulphur dioxide. As soon as fermentation is established the must can be transferred to a demijohn and the mead making process continued exactly as described earlier under the heat sterilizing method.

Fining

After fermentation is complete and the mead has been racked it should, if placed in a cool position, become brilliantly clear in a few months. If it remains cloudy put the demijohn in a much colder place, such as an outdoor shed or garage, and it will usually be found that clearing is accelerated. Sometimes, despite this treatment, the mead remains hazy and it is then necessary to do something more. The theory as to why a wine remains cloudy is that the tiny floating particles carry an electrical charge which is the same on all the particles, either positive or negative, and as like charges repel, the particles will not aggregate together and therefore remain in suspension. A fining agent has particles with a neutralising opposite electrical charge. When introduced into the mead they will attract the particles causing the haze, combine with them to form larger heavier bodies which by the force of gravity will deposit in the bottom of the jar.

There are a number of fining agents available. Some are inorganic minerals such as Bentonite, Kaolin, Silica, Charcoal etc. whilst others are complex organic substances such as Egg White, Milk Casein, Gelatine, Isinglass etc. The amateur wine maker is advised to purchase a proprietary fining agent and follow the instructions provided.

After adding the fining agent, the mead should be left to stand in the cold for a couple of days and will then benefit by being filtered. This can be done through filter paper in a funnel but it is important to obtain good quality filter paper from a wine makers shop because it is essential not to use paper which might leave a taste. An easily available alternative is to use filter paper which is sold in supermarkets for use in coffee making machines. Whatever filter paper is used it is a wise precaution to run a gallon of cold clean water through it before use to make sure that it does not leave a taste in the mead. After filtering, a Campden tablet should be added to the wine to ensure that the procedure has not introduced contaminants.

Although fining and filtration may sometimes be required it must be emphasized that a well made balanced mead should clear naturally in a cool situation without such interference.

CHAPTER 5

MAKING LARGER QUANTITIES OF MEAD

In the previous chapter a method of making one gallon of mead has been described in some detail. Although the principles of wine making remain unchanged, some modification of method is usually required when a larger volume of must is involved. For example, a beekeeper with a modest apiary of ten productive colonies should expect to harvest a quarter of a ton of honey in a reasonable season. In the extraction of this quantity much honey will be left in the extractor, settling tank, uncapping tray, buckets etc. which can be usefully retrieved for making mead. By washing out all apparatus carefully with clean cold water several gallons of good quality must can be obtained and processed as follows.

Wash out all apparatus with clean cold drinking water. The volume of water required will vary, of course, with the size of the equipment but usually two or three gallons will be needed. These original washings will contain many pieces of wax, dead bees etc. which should be removed by filtering through muslin into a fermentation bin. In addition, after draining as much honey as possible from them, cappings can be washed and will yield a surprising quantity of honey.

When these washings have been collected into a clean fermentation bin it is now vitally necessary to determine the specific gravity by the use of a hydrometer and from the reading obtained calculate the weight of honey per gallon by reference to the Gravity Table in the previous chapter. The best starting specific gravity is 1.100; if it is much higher the yeast will be inhibited. If a higher reading is obtained, as is usually the case, the washings will need to be diluted by the addition of more clean water until the specific gravity is reduced to the recommended starting figure. If, on the other hand, the washings are found to have a specific gravity which is too low then more honey will need to be added. Obviously, it is desirable to start with such a volume of water which will produce washings high in honey content which need diluting, rather than having to add precious honey to bring a weak must up to strength.

Having adjusted the washings to the recommended starting specific gravity it is convenient to transfer to a five gallon fermentation bin. Larger bins when full are a struggle to lift! To five gallons of must are added acid (25g Citric, 25g Tartaric, 25g Malic), five teaspoons of yeast nutrient, a teaspoon of dried grape tannin, 500mg Vitamin C and five 3mg tablets of Vitamin B_1.

If the volume of washings is less, or more than five gallons then the above quantities of additives must be adjusted proportionately,

A practical tip is to crush the vitamin tablets and mix with all the other ingredients (dry) before adding to the must. If this is not done and the tannin is added separately it tends to float on the surface and is difficult to incorporate.

The must should now be sterilized by the addition of 5 crushed Campden tablets. If the volume is less than five gallons use one Campden tablet per gallon.

The bin should be covered with a clean cloth and placed in a warm position, preferably at about 70°F (21°C). If a warm position is not available the must can be maintained at a suitable temperature by use of a heating cable wrapped around the outside of the fermentation bin. A type which is readily available in the UK and reasonably priced is marketed under the name 'Brewbelt'. Mine have given many years of good service.

After 72 hours the must should be stirred and vigorously agitated with a large spoon so as to expel as much sulphur dioxide as possible and at the same time introduce atmospheric oxygen. The yeast which has been activated in a starter bottle is then introduced.

During the next 72 hours the must should be kept warm and stirred occasionally. When fermentation has started, as indicated by froth and bubbles appearing on the surface of the must, it should be transferred to a fermentation receptacle into which an air lock is fitted. Alternatively the must can be transferred into an appropriate number of one gallon demijohns, each of which must have an air lock. Thereafter subsequent care is as described in the previous chapter. If allowed to ferment out a dry mead will result but if a sweet beverage is required further honey will have to be added as previously described.

CHAPTER 6

FRUIT AND SPICED MEADS

Mixing fruit and spices with mead has a very long history, the practice being well documented in Greek and Roman times. Perhaps the uncharitable and cynical may suggest that because the process of fermentation was not understood in those early times, the beverages produced were so poor that they required the addition of fruit juices and spices to make them palatable! Whatever the truth may be about the origin of the practice there can be no argument that many interesting drinks can be produced by fermenting fruit juices and spices with honey.

It has a certain charm that those distinct wines are still known today by the following ancient names.

Melomel - a wine produced by fermenting a fruit juice (other than grape) with honey

Pyment - red or white - a wine produced from grape juice and honey

Hippocras - a wine from grape juice, herbs and honey

Cyser- a wine from fermenting apple juice with honey

Metheglin- mead flavoured with spices.

Top quality pure mead, which has a delicate and distinctive aroma and flavour, is not easy to produce and most beginners find it easier to produce a drinkable melomel. For example, when strongly flavoured fruit such as blackcurrants are used in melomel, minor deficiencies in the fermentation will be masked by the wonderful aroma and flavour of the fruit.

Recipes for various fruit wines will be given in a later chapter. However, there are a number of general points applicable to brewing fruit wines which will be made here in order to avoid repetition in the individual recipes.

Good quality wines can be made from commercial canned concentrated grape and fruit juices. If fresh fruit, such as grapes are used, it is important that they are of a variety suitable for wine making because the common dessert types do not make good wine. Grapes and soft fruit should be pressed and only the juice used.

Firmer fruits, such as gooseberries, plums, apples etc. which may be difficult to press should be mechanically pulped. When placed in the appropriate volume of water for the must, juice extraction from the pulped fruit can be facilitated by the addition of Rohamet-P, an enzyme preparation which breaks down the cell walls of fruit. It should be used according to the makers instructions.

Fruit juices contain quantities of pectins, which are polysaccharides derived from plant cell walls. They may cause an undesirable haze in the finished wine ('pectin haze'). The problem can be avoided by addition to the must of the enzyme pectolase which breaks down pectin. Both of these enzyme products are available from wine makers shops and are not expensive.

All musts containing fruit or fruit juices should be cold sterilized because heating will enormously increase the pectin concentration.

Some fruits do not combine well with honey and are best avoided. For example, blackberries and elderberries have an excess of tannin and produce very astringent melomels which most people dislike.

All melomels and cyser benefit from incorporating into the recipe half a can of white grape concentrate per gallon. This greatly improves the body and 'vinosity' of the wine, as will also the inclusion of a couple of mashed very ripe bananas.

Although the individual items and quantities will vary in the different recipes, the general principles of brewing melomels will be similar. The following method for making Redcurrant Melomel is described in detail as a guiding example.

Redcurrant Melomel (sweet)

Ingredients

3 lb (1.36 kg) light or medium honey
3 lb (1.36 kg) redcurrants
Half can (0.5 kg) white grape concentrate
2 very ripe bananas
1 teaspoon yeast nutrient

1 teaspoon of pectolase
1 gallon water
Pommard yeast
Campden tablet

Method

Wash the fruit and remove from the stalks. Place the fruit in a fermentation bin or clean bucket and crush (the kitchen implement used for mashing potatoes is useful for this purpose). Dissolve two pounds of honey in about five pints of water, add the half can of grape concentrate, the yeast nutrient, pectolase and then add to the fruit in the fermentation bin.

Stir in one crushed Campden tablet Cover the bin with a clean cloth and leave for 24 to 48 hours in the warm. At the end of this period stir the must vigorously for a few minutes to dispel sulphur dioxide before adding the yeast which has been brought into activity in a starter bottle as described in the earlier chapter. If kept in the warm, fermentation should become apparent in about 48 to 72 hours. The fruit will rise to the surface of the must forming a cap. This should be broken up twice daily by stirring. Ferment on the pulp for 5 days (i.e. 5 days of visible active fermentation) then strain through muslin to remove the pulp. Transfer to a demijohn, fit an airlock, top up with water but leave sufficient space for the addition of further honey, and keep in the warm - 60°F to 65°F. Test the specific gravity regularly and when it has fallen to 1.005 add four ounces of the remaining honey. Repeat this process until all the honey is used. When fermentation ceases taste the melomel and if too dry add a little more honey. Repeat this procedure until fermentation has finally stopped and the melomel suits your palate as regards sweetness. When a deposit has formed in the bottom of the demijohn, rack into a clean jar, top up with water if necessary and add a Campden tablet.

Store in a cool place, rack again if further significant deposit develops. Be patient because it will take two or three years for your melomel to mature fully!

Fermenting bin and demijohn with air lock

Simple Siphon system for racking

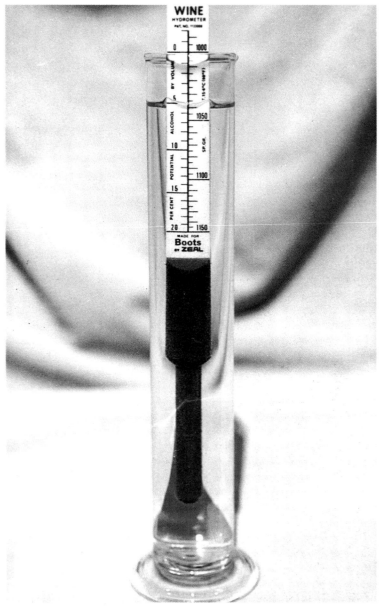

Hydrometer and jar. Miniscus shows SG = 1040

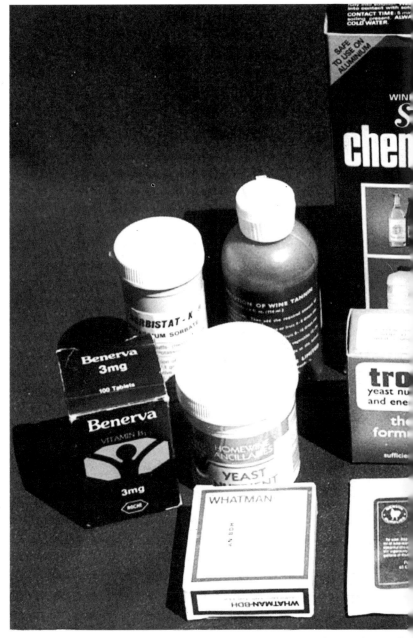

Common items used in mead making. Alongside

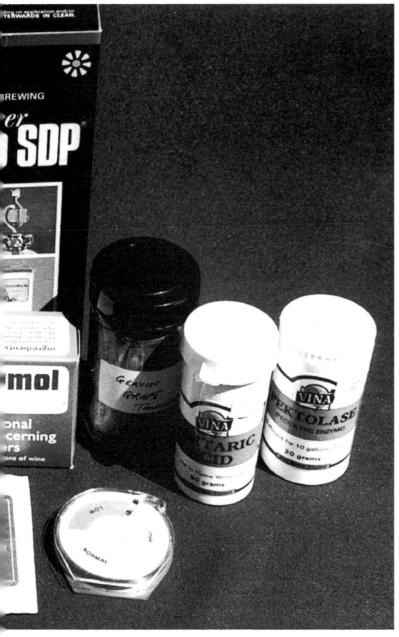

t of yeast at the front are rolls of acidity testing paper

Wine glasses. On the left, an unsuitable shape for tasting.
On the right, the correctly shaped ISO
(International Standards Organisation) tasting glass.

CHAPTER 7

STORING, BOTTLING, LABELLING, SERVING

Storing

Mead, like all wines, should be stored in a cool place at 50°F to 55°F, in the dark, and free from excessive vibration. A cellar is an ideal place. Obviously, perfect conditions are not available to everyone and many cope adequately by storing in garages or somewhere similar.

Under no circumstances should wine be stored in a roof loft because it will become far too hot in summer.

The author finds it convenient to keep mead in demijohns and bottle when required for use. If stored in bottle, remember to lay the bottles on their sides so as to keep the corks moist. The disadvantage of bottle storage is that if the mead continues to throw a deposit, this will settle up the side of the bottle making decanting a little tricky if a cloudy wine is to be avoided. When stored in a demijohn the deposit falls to the bottom of the jar and it is easy to siphon off five bottles of wine without disturbing the deposit leaving perhaps only the sixth bottle a little cloudy.

Whether stored in demijohns or bottles the mead should fill such containers to within half an inch of the bottom of the bung or cork so that there is a minimum of air space present. It is important to exclude as much air as possible so as to prevent oxidation.

If several demijohns of mead are made in a season, or are accumulated over a period of time, it is very unlikely that they will be identical even though a similar brewing method was observed. There are a number of possible explanations but the most important one is that honey, the main ingredient, is variable and this obviously affects the final result. It is, therefore, desirable to taste the mead before final storage. If one batch is a little lacking in acid it can be blended with another which has an excess; similarly, if one jar is too sweet it can be blended with another which is not sweet enough, and so on. Blending is an important activity which is an integral part of the commercial wine industry.

After blending different batches of mead it is wise to add a Campden tablet to each jar and observe for a week or two to make sure that the wine is stable and that fermentation has not re-started.

Mead, like all good wine, matures and improves with age. As a simple rule of thumb, I believe that dry mead should be stored for at least two years and a good sweet mead not less than five years.

Bottling

Mead should not be bottled until it is stable and brilliantly clear. If, after a year in a demijohn it is not completely clear, it should be moved to a colder place. This will usually solve the problem. If, however, it does not, and the mead remains cloudy, then the only alternative is to fine and filter as previously described in chapter four.

Standard 75cl green wine bottles are appropriate for mead. They must be washed carefully and sterilized by rinsing with a metabisulphite solution made by dissolving two Campden tablets with a pinch of citric acid in one pint of water.

Corks should be of the best quality and should be soaked in metabisulphite solution for 24 hours before use.

A hand corking implement will be required. When the cork is fully inserted into the bottle not more than half an inch of air space should remain between the surface of the wine and the bottom of the cork.

When filled and corked the bottles should be stored on their sides to ensure that the corks remain moist. If a cork dries it is likely to allow air to permeate through it into the bottle.

Plastic corks are being used more frequently for cheaper commercial wines. They are quite satisfactory providing a good tight fit is achieved.

Labelling

A good mead which has taken much time and effort to produce

deserves to be presented nicely. There can be no doubt that a professionally printed colourful label on a bottle conveys an impression of quality and enhances the anticipation of the imbiber. On the other hand, a scruffy hand written label encourages the critical attitude that the mead is of such doubtful quality that it doesn't merit a decent label!

Desirable information on a label should be (a) an indication of what the bottle contains i.e. 'Mead – Sweet', or 'Mead – Dry' etc.; (b) the year it was made; and (c) the name of the producer.

The corks on bottles should be sealed with capsules. These protect the corks and also give the bottles a finished 'professional' look. A simple inexpensive plastic type is available which contracts to a tight fit when exposed to steam from the spout of a boiling kettle.

Serving

If the mead has been stored in a bottle, correctly laying on its side, it is helpful to stand the bottle upright for 48 hours before use so that any deposit will accumulate in the punted bottom of the bottle and be less likely to be disturbed when the wine is poured. If there is much deposit present the mead should be carefully decanted before use.

All meads, melomels etc. should be chilled before serving. The classical way is by standing in a bucket of ice but an hour in a refrigerator will do equally well.

The wine should be drunk from a plain glass tulip shaped goblet. The tulip shape being important as it helps to retain the bouquet (or 'nose') of the wine.

Dry meads and melomels go well with food but many find that the sweeter varieties are more acceptable as 'social wines' to be drunk on their own. This is obviously a matter of individual preference.

CHAPTER 8

PROBLEMS

The golden rules of wine making are (a) maintain the highest standard of sterility of equipment and (b) avoid exposure of wine to air. If these rules are followed much trouble will be prevented. However, a beginner may encounter occasional difficulties, of which the following are the most common.

Stuck Fermentation
When an active yeast is added to a must which has been cold sterilized it may take two or three days before fermentation becomes obvious because the residual sulphur dioxide in the must slows down yeast growth. However, if after three days there is no sign of fermentation, check that the temperature of the must is somewhere between 60°F and 70°F. If the temperature is correct, vigorously stir the must to introduce air and expel sulphur dioxide, and leave in the warm for a further 48 hours. Usually fermentation will then become obvious but if it does not the best action is to add fresh active yeast together with an additional spoonful of yeast nutrient.

Occasionally, fermentation will start satisfactorily and then cease long before all the honey in the must has been converted into alcohol. The fermentation is then described as having stuck. The condition can be suspected if bubbles are absent from the must and can be verified by the use of the hydrometer. If the Specific Gravity is greater than 1.025, and ceases to fall after a further week, it can be assumed that fermentation has ceased.

Fermentation can stick for a number of reasons. Sometimes the temperature of the must is too high or too low; there may be an inadequate supply of nutrients and acid; there may be an excessively high concentration of sugar; or excessive residual sulphur dioxide. Very rarely fermentation stops because the alcohol content has reached a level which inhibits the yeast.

A must which has stuck can be very difficult to re-start. Probably the best action is to prepare a fresh active yeast in a starter bottle and add it to half a demijohn of the inactive must. Check that the Specific Gravity of the must is not greater than 1.035. If it is, dilute with water down to this reading. Add an extra spoonful of yeast nutrient and the juice from half a lemon. Insert an airlock in the jar and when fermentation is vigorous gradually fill the demijohn by adding some of the inactive must every other day until the new jar is full.

Failure to clear

When fermentation is complete, mead will often be very slow to clear if kept too warm. The first step to clear a cloudy mead, therefore, is to put it in a cold place such as an outside shed or garage. This will usually solve the problem in two or three weeks. If the mead does not become brilliantly clear in that time then the remaining action is to fine and filter.

In melomels and other fruit wines the presence of pectins can cause a persisting haze. The only remedy is to treat with a pectolase enzyme and fine and filter.

Oxidation

Throughout all stages of wine making it is important to exclude air as much as is feasibly possible. When wine is exposed to air, small quantities of alcohol are oxidised to acetaldehyde and acetic acid. To a very limited extent this does not matter, and in some circumstances may be considered part of the maturing process of wine, but if it goes on in excess the wine will taste flat and lifeless and white wines will darken. An oxidised mead will never win on the show bench.

Acetification

A group of bacteria known as *Acetobacter* can infect wine and have the disastrous effect of converting alcohol into acetic acid. In everyday language they change wine into vinegar. Acetobacter are opportunistic contaminants which thrive in warm conditions with plenty of air. They are inhibited by high alcohol concentration and sulphur dioxide.

Wine which has become vinegar cannot, quite obviously, be salvaged. The only action the wine maker can take is to prevent the problem by not exposing wine to air, maintaining high standards of sterility, and the prudent use of Campden tablets at the appropriate stages of the brewing processes.

Off Flavours

Sometimes insufficient acid in the must will cause mead to have a medicinal flavour. Prevent the problem by using the correct amount of acid at the start because little can be done when a pronounced flavour has developed.

A large group of micro-organisms known as lactic acid bacteria can be responsible for off flavours. They can also cause a peculiar ropiness or oiliness of the wine and sometimes a nasty bitter flavour. There is little that can be done when such problems have developed. It is necessary to repeat once more that prevention is required by the judicious use of Campden tablets during the brewing processes because all these bacteria are suppressed by sulphur dioxide.

CHAPTER 9

RECIPES

The following recipes are given as examples of the wide variety of wines which can be made with honey. The list is intended to be illustrative and not exhaustive. Furthermore, it is not suggested that the results will suit everyone because palates vary enormously. However, the recipes are reasonably simple and should produce drinkable beverages. It is strongly recommended that when experience has been gained the wine maker should experiment and develop recipes which suit his own palate.

Dry Mead

Ingredients

3 lbs (1.36 kg) light honey
6 pints (3.37 litres) water
1 teaspoon yeast nutrient
$\frac{1}{4}$ teaspoon grape tannin (or 2 tablespoons of cold strong tea)
Vitamin B₁ tablet
Juice of a lemon (or citric, tartaric and malic acids, level teaspoon of each)
Chablis yeast

Method

Method as described previously in Chapter four. Dissolve the honey in the water in a clean sterile fermentation bucket. Mix in the yeast nutrient, crushed Vitamin B₁ tablet, grape tannin and lemon juice (or acid). Add a crushed Campden tablet to sterilize. Cover with a clean cloth and place in the warm. After 48 hours agitate vigorously with a large spoon to expel sulphur dioxide and add the yeast which has been brought into activity in a starter bottle. Cover and keep warm. When fermentation is observed transfer to a demijohn into which an airlock is inserted. Top up the jar to within an inch of the bung when fermentation become less vigorous. Continue fermentation to dryness at a temperature between 60°F (15°C) and 70°F (21°C).

After completion of fermentation rack into a clean demijohn, add one Campden tablet and store in the cool. Rack again later if significant deposit forms. Keep for 1 to 2 years before drinking.

Sweet Mead

Ingredients
  4 to 4¼ lbs (1.81 to 2 kg) honey (light, medium or heather)
  6 pints (3.37 litres) water
  1 teaspoon yeast nutrient
  ¼ teaspoon grape tannin
  Vitamin B₁ tablet
  Level teaspoon of each of the three acids, citric, tartaric, and malic (total 15g)
  Sauterne or Tokay yeast

Method
The method has been fully described in Chapter four. To repeat very briefly, follow the same procedure as described for dry mead making up the original must with 3 lbs (1.36 kg) of honey. After the stage of transfer to the demijohn, check the Specific Gravity every 3 or 4 days and when it falls to 1.005 add a further 4 oz (115g approximately) of honey. Repeat the additions of honey when the SG again falls to 1.005 until all the honey is used or fermentation stops. It is desirable after the last addition of honey, if fermentation is still continuing, to stop it by the addition of two crushed Campden tablets when the SG has fallen to something between 1.010 and 1.015. After a few days rack from the lees into a clean sterile jar, top up with water to within an inch of the bung, and store in the cool. Rack in subsequent months as required. A good full bodied sweet mead needs at least three years to mature.

Sparkling Mead

Ingredients
As for dry mead with the exception that a champagne yeast would be preferred.

Method
Proceed as described previously for dry mead. When fermentation in the demijohn has progressed to almost dryness, i.e. specific gravity below 1.005, add about ½ lb (227 g) of honey to the jar and mix well. Replace the airlock, put in the warm and after a few days when fermentation is seen to be active, rack the mead into champagne bottles leaving an air space of about 1 inches. Cork firmly with champagne-type plastic stoppers, obtainable from winemaking equipment suppliers. The corks must be wired in position. The bottles should be stored on their sides at a temperature of about 60°F (15°C) for at least six months before opening.

It must be emphasized that only heavy champagne bottles should be used because ordinary wine bottles cannot stand the internal pressure created by the carbon dioxide and could explode causing serious injury.

White Pyment
(a) Using natural grape juice
It is important to use varieties of grapes suited to wine making. Dessert grapes are deficient in acid and do not make good wine. About twenty pounds (9 kg) of grapes will be required to produce seven pints of juice.
Ingredients
   7 pints (4 litres) of grape juice
   2 lbs (1 kg) light or medium honey
   Chablis yeast
Method
Extract the juice from the grapes by crushing and pressing. Add the honey and stir until dissolved. Place in a demijohn, add a crushed Campden tablet, stir, leave in the warm for 24 hours. After 24 hours have elapsed add the active yeast culture. Fit an airlock and place the jar where it will not be too warm, i.e. not more than 60°F to 65°F because yeast thrives in natural grape juice and there is some risk that fermentation may become too vigorous causing frothing and overflow from the jar. If fermentation becomes very vigorous move the jar into a cool position.

When fermentation is complete, rack into a clean sterile jar, add a Campden tablet and store in the cool. Subsequently, rack again if more deposit forms. Pyment should be kept for two years before use.

(b) Using grape concentrate

Tinned white grape concentrate is widely available for wine making. Full instructions are given on the label and very often a packet of yeast is included. To make pyment, follow the instructions on the tin, substituting 1.25 lbs of honey for each pound of sugar in the recipe.

Red Pyment

Is best made using tinned red grape concentrate. Follow the instructions given on the label remembering to substitute 1.25 lbs of honey for each pound of sugar in the recipe.

MELOMELS

A wide range of fresh fruits, dried fruits and fruit juices, can be fermented with honey to produce acceptable wines. Some are suitable for both dry and sweet wines whilst others are good in one style and not so attractive in the other. A few fruits have special characteristics which can cause difficulty, perhaps the most common being the blackberry. This particular fruit has a very high tannin content which makes young wine very astringent. With time in bottle the problem should resolve but it may take some years! For this reason if blackberries are included in a recipe the quantity should be carefully limited.

Peach Melomel - (Sweet)

Ingredients

    4 lbs (1.8 kg) ripe peaches

    2 to 3lbs (0.9 to 1.36 kg) light or medium honey

    ½ Can (0.5 kg) white grape concentrate

    ¼ teaspoon grape tannin

    Juice of a lemon

    1 teaspoon yeast nutrient

    Pectolase

    Rohamet P

    Vitamin B1 tablet

    Sauterne yeast

    Water to 1 gallon

Method
Quarter the peaches and remove the stones. Place in a fermentation bucket and cover with five pints of cold water. Add 1 lb of honey, the grape concentrate, lemon juice, grape tannin, yeast nutrient, crushed Vitamin B_1 tablet, pectolase and Rohamet P. Use pectolase and Rohamet P in the amounts as recommended by the makers. Stir well and add one crushed Campden tablet. Cover with a clean cloth and place in the warm. After 48 hours stir well and add the yeast which has been activated in a starter bottle. Stir twice daily and allow to ferment on the pulp for about five days. Then strain through clean fine mesh cloth into a demijohn, top up with water, fit an airlock and keep warm. Check the Specific gravity with a hydrometer and when the SG falls below 1010 add 4 ozs of honey. Stir. Continue adding 4oz increments of honey each time the SG falls below 1010 until fermentation stops, preferably within the SG range of 1010 to 1020. Add a crushed Campden tablet and rack into a clean jar. Rack subsequently when significant deposit forms.

Keep for at least two years. The melomel produced by this method is best drunk as a social wine.

Blackcurrant Melomel (Sweet)

Ingredients
    3 lbs (1.36 kg) blackcurrants
    1 lb (0.45 kg) very ripe bananas
    ½ can red grape concentrate
    3 lbs (1.36 kg) medium honey
    Juice of ½ lemon
    1 teaspoon yeast nutrient
    1 Vitamin B_1 tablet
    ¼ spoon grape tannin
    Pectolase
    Rohamet P
    All Purpose Wine yeast
    Water to 1 gallon

Method
Remove the blackcurrants from their stalks and place in the fermentation vessel with the skinned bananas. Crush the fruit. Add about 5 pints of water, one crushed Campden tablet together with

the pectolase and Rohamet P. Stir, cover and leave in the warm 48 hours. After that add 1 lb honey, the yeast nutrient, tannin, crushed vitamin B1 tablet, lemon juice and the half can of grape concentrate. Stir well before adding the yeast which has been activated in a starter bottle. Cover the vessel and keep in the warm. When active fermentation is observed allow to ferment on the pulp for a further three days. Then strain from the pulp through a fine mesh cloth into a demijohn. Add 1 lb of honey and stir to mix. Top up the jar with water, fit an airlock and place in the warm (65°F). When the Specific Gravity has fallen to 1.005 add 4 oz of honey dissolved in some of the fermenting must taken from the jar. Repeat this process until all the honey has been used, or fermentation has ceased. When fermentation is complete rack into a clean jar, top up to within an inch of the bung, add a crushed Campden tablet and store in the cool. Rack subsequently if further deposit forms.

Sweet blackcurrant melomel should be allowed to mature for two or three years.

Raspberry Melomel
Ingredients
   3 lbs (1.36 kg) raspberries
   3 lbs (1.36 kg) medium honey
   1 lb (0.45 kg) very ripe bananas
   1/2 can white grape concentrate
   1/4 teaspoon grape tannin
   1 teaspoon yeast nutrient
   Juice of 1/2 lemon
   1 Vitamin B1 tablet
   Pectolase
   Rohamet P
   Water to 1 gallon
   Sauterne yeast
Method
As described for blackcurrant melomel. Only dry good quality raspberries should be used. Allow the wine to mature for two years.

Damson Melomel
This can be made either dry or sweet. If being made sweet allow an additional 1 lb of honey.

Ingredients
  4 lbs (1.81 kg) damsons
  3 lbs (1.36 kg) medium honey
  ½ can red grape concentrate
  1 teaspoon yeast nutrient
  ¼ teaspoon grape tannin
  2 teaspoons citric acid
  1 Vitamin B₁ tablet
  Pectolase
  Rohamet P
  Burgundy or Bordeaux yeast
  Water to 1 gallon
Method
Wash and stalk the damsons. Place in a fermentation bin and pour on six pints of boiling water. When cool mash the fruit and remove the stones. Add the acid, tannin, pectolase, Rohamet P, yeast nutrient, crushed Vitamin B₁ tablet and one crushed Campden tablet. Cover and leave in the warm for 24 hours. After that stir well and add the grape concentrate, 2lbs of honey and activated yeast. Cover and ferment in the warm for one week, stirring daily to break up the fruit cap, then strain into a demijohn, add the remaining pound of honey, top up with water and fit an airlock. Ferment to dryness in the warm, then rack into a clean jar, add a Campden tablet and store in the cool.

If a sweet wine is intended then after straining into the demijohn, having added the third pound of honey, keep a check on the Specific Gravity with a hydrometer. When the SG falls below 1.010 add 4 ozs of honey. Keep checking the SG and each time it falls below 1.010 add a further 4ozs of honey until the total allocated quantity is used. After the last addition aim to stop fermentation when the SG is about 1.010 by racking and adding two crushed Campden tablets.

Sweet damson melomel matures slowly and needs to be kept at least two years.

Apricot – Fresh Fruit
Ingredients and method exactly the same as described for Peach Melomel, substituting apricots for the peaches.
Apricot – Dried fruit
Can be made sweet or dry.

Ingredients
    1 lb (0.45 kg) dried apricots
    1 lb (0.45 kg) very ripe bananas
    ½ can white grape concentrate
    3 lbs (1.36 kg) light or medium honey
    2 teaspoons citric acid (or juice of a lemon)
    ¼ teaspoon grape tannin
    1 teaspoon yeast nutrient
    1 Vitamin B1 tablet
    Pectolase
    Rohamet P
    Sauterne yeast for sweet, All Purpose wine yeast for dry
    Water to 1 gallon
Method
Chop the apricots and soak in 4 pints of water overnight. The next day simmer the apricots for five minutes and allow to cool. When cool add the skinned bananas and crush. Add the grape concentrate, acid, tannin, yeast nutrient, crushed Vitamin B1 tablet, pectolase and Rohamet P. Cover and keep warm. The next day stir in 2 lbs of honey and the active yeast culture. Ferment on the pulp for 7 days, stirring daily to break up the fruit cap. After that strain into a clean demijohn add the remaining pound of honey, fit an airlock and ferment to dryness.

If a sweet wine is required proceed to add additional honey as described in the recipe for sweet damson melomel.

Redcurrant

This can be made sweet or dry.
Ingredients
    3 lbs (1.36 kg) redcurrants
    ½ can white grape concentrate
    3 lbs (1.36 kg) light or medium honey
    1 teaspoon yeast nutrient
    1 Vitamin B1 tablet
    Pectolase
    Bordeaux yeast
    Water to 1 gallon
Method
Use ripe, good quality fruit. Remove fruit from the green stalks as

the latter, if included, will impart a bitterness to the wine. Place the fruit in the fermentation bin with six pints of water and mash . Add a crushed Campden tablet and the pectolase, cover and place in the warm. The next day add the grape concentrate, yeast nutrient, Vitamin B₁ tablet, two pounds of honey and the active yeast culture. Ferment on the pulp for five days, stirring daily, and then strain into a clean demijohn, add the remaining pound of honey, fit an airlock and ferment to dryness in the warm.

If a sweet wine is required proceed to add additional honey as described in the recipe for sweet damson melomel

Gooseberry (Dry)

Ingredients

    3 lbs (1.36 kg) gooseberries (the green variety, nearly ripe)
    ¹/₂ can white grape concentrate
    3 lbs (1.36 kg) light or medium honey
    1 teaspoon yeast nutrient
    ¹/₄ teaspoon grape tannin
    1 Vitamin B₁ tablet
    Pectolase
    Rohamet P
    Water to 1 gallon
    Chablis yeast

Method

Top, tail and wash the gooseberries. Place in a fermentation bin and pour on six pints of boiling water. When cool crush the fruit, add the pectolase, Rohamet P and one crushed Campden tablet. Leave for 24 hours then stir in the grape concentrate, 2 lbs of honey, yeast nutrient, tannin, crushed Vitamin B₁ tablet and the yeast which has been activated in a starter bottle. Ferment on the pulp for five days, stirring daily. After that strain into a demijohn which contains the remaining one pound of honey. Top up with cold water, fit an airlock and ferment to dryness

Gooseberry (Sweet)

The same basic ingredients as above but an extra 1 lb of honey will be required. A Tokay yeast would be more suitable.

The method is the same as for the dry wine but the extra honey is added in 4oz increments as the SG falls, in the same way as described in the recipe for sweet damson melomel.

CYSER

Cyser is a wine made from apple juice and honey. Undoubtedly, it is less laborious to purchase and use prepared apple juice, but those with apple trees will probably wish to utilize the fresh fruit which they may have in excess. Recipes for both methods are given.

Cyser (1)

Ingredients

    4 pints (2.25 l) pure apple juice
    $2\frac{1}{2}$ lbs (1.1 kg) medium or light honey
    $\frac{1}{2}$ can white grape concentrate
    $\frac{1}{2}$ teaspoon citric acid
    Pectolase
    $\frac{1}{4}$ teaspoon grape tannin
    1 teaspoon yeast nutrient
    1 Vitamin B_1 tablet
    Chablis yeast
    Water to one gallon

Method

Mix all the ingredients in a fermentation bin in the warm using an active yeast culture. Transfer to a demijohn, fit an airlock but leave 4 inches of air space initially. When the first vigorous fermentation has settled the jar can be topped up with water. Keep in the warm and ferment to dryness.

Cyser (2) Using fresh fruit.

(a) If a fruit press or juice extractor is available then prepare six pints of juice and proceed as in Cyser (1) above. The apples used should be ripe, clean and wholesome. A mixture of desert and cooking varieties helps to balance the natural acidity.

(b) Pulp fermentation.

Ingredients

    10 lbs (4.5 kg) apples
    $\frac{1}{2}$ can white grape concentrate
    3 lbs (1.36 kg) medium or light honey
    1 teaspoon yeast nutrient
    1 Vitamin B_1 tablet

1 teaspoon citric acid
Pectolase
Rohamet P
Chablis or Tokay yeast
Water to 1 gallon

Method

Pour 4 pints of cold water into the fermentation bin and stir in the citric acid, pectolase, Rohamet P and one crushed Campden tablet.

Wash the apples, remove any bad or bruised parts but do not peel or core. Cut the apples into small segments and drop into the fermentation bin quickly so as to avoid browning. Cover and place in the warm for 24 hours.

Next day stir in the grape concentrate, 1 lb of honey, yeast nutrient, crushed Vitamin B_1 tablet and the activated yeast culture. Cover and ferment on the pulp in the warm for seven days, stirring daily to break up the fruit cap. At the end of this period strain into a demijohn containing the remaining 2 lbs of honey, top up with water, fit an airlock and ferment in the warm to dryness. Rack as necessary and store in the cool to mature for two years.

HIPPOCRAS

Hippocras is pyment to which herbs and spices have been added. The name apparently derives from Hippocrates (*c.*460-357 BC), the most famous early Greek physician.

Method

Prepare pyment as described earlier. When fermentation is complete rack into a clean demijohn. Make a small muslin bag into which the spices can be placed. This is then suspended on strong thread in the pyment and the jar sealed. The beverage should be tasted every three or four days and the spices removed when an acceptable flavour has been achieved. Spices such as ginger, cinnamon, orange and lemon peel, cloves etc. may be used. Very little is required to flavour one gallon of wine.

METHEGLIN

Metheglin is spiced mead, it can be made sweet or dry.

Method

Prepare mead as described earlier and introduce spices in exactly the same way as described in the preparation of hippocras.

Remember that the flavour of the spices should not be strong and overpowering.

CHAPTER 10

EXHIBITING

It is interesting to speculate on why amateur beekeepers devote so much time and effort in preparing exhibits of honey, wax, and mead etc.for honey shows. There is little financial reward for such activity so it must be assumed that the motivation has something to do with a competitive urge and or, satisfaction (vanity?) in having the excellence of their produce acknowledged. Whatever the explanation, honey shows and competitions have an excellent beneficial effect in that they raise the standards of preparation and presentation of apicultural products.

If you contemplate entering mead in a show the first essential is to study very carefully the show schedule and decide which classes to enter. Very small local shows may only have one class for mead but most will have separate classes for sweet and dry types. Larger shows will also have classes for melomels etc.

At the outset, before selecting your exhibits, it is important to confirm from your records that the mead you intend to show is 'pure' in the sense that it has been made solely from honey, water, acid, tannin, yeast nutrient and yeast. No other additives are allowed. It is not permissible to add artificial sweeteners or sugar, nor may it be laced with vodka or brandy etc.!

When sampling and selecting your potential exhibits, ruthlessly discard any which in your judgement are not up to standard. There is no point in exhibiting rubbish.

The first decision is to decide whether your mead should be entered in the 'dry' or the 'sweet' class. An experienced taster can determine this immediately but the novice should use a hydrometer. A dry mead should have a Specific Gravity of 1.000 or less, whilst for a sweet mead the Specific Gravity should be somewhere between 1.010 and 1.020. The category 'dry' seems to cause the most problems for exhibitors because if the schedule states 'Dry mead' then the exhibit **must** be dry without any trace of sweetness. It cannot be 'medium dry'. To illustrate the problem, a few years ago it was my unhappy duty at a very large County Show to disqualify a whole class of dry mead because none of the exhibits was dry. The local steward who was helping me thought this tough decision was likely to cause some argument so, to make the position quite clear and forestall trouble, I used my hydrometer on every exhibit and recorded the reading on each bottle. All were well above a Specific Gravity of 1.000. Fortunately, that distinguished County Association has remained friendly towards me and in subsequent years I have been invited back to judge again!

The following is a suggested step by step sequence for preparing an exhibit for a show.

1. Select the mead.

Assuming that the mead has been stored to mature in a demijohn, it should be brilliantly bright and clear with no floating particles. If there is floating debris the wine can be filtered but this should be avoided if possible because filtering introduces too much air and diminishes the natural aroma. It should have an attractive colour, dark yellow or straw hues are good. The aroma should be clean and fresh with no smell of sulphur dioxide. On tasting, the mead should show a good balance of flavour, acidity, astringency and alcohol. Dry mead should be clean and fresh in the mouth. Sweet mead should be clearly sweet but not sickly sweet. It should have a higher alcohol content than a dry mead and a more pronounced aroma.

2. Bottles and corks

The show schedule will usually stipulate the size and type of bottle to be used and the style of cork. For example, the National Honey Show in London currently requires mead to be shown in clear colourless or slightly green tinged glass punted bottles of round section of approximately 26 fluid ounces capacity, with rounded not sloping shoulders and without lettering, fluting or ornamentation of any kind. Only cork stoppers with white plastic flanges may be used. Such instructions must be followed precisely.

Bottles should be free from chips and cracks and try to ensure that there are no faults or blemishes in the glass. Wash the bottles carefully using a bottle brush to ensure that the punted bottom is absolutely clean. Rinse out with cold boiled water and allow to dry in a warm oven.

Always use a new cork and one which is without cracks or blemishes.

3. *Bottling*

This is best done a few days before the show so that the mead has time to settle and regenerate its full aroma, which may be temporarily impaired by the process of bottling.

Place the demijohn on a box, or something similar, so as to raise it about two feet in height above the table on which the bottling is to be done. There are a number of proprietary siphon tubes on the market but a three feet length of plastic tubing, of not more than about $\frac{1}{8}$ inch bore, is really all that is necessary. Prior to use it should be sterilised by immersion in boiling water.

Remove the bung from the storage jar and carefully pass one end of the tubing into the mead so that the inlet is about one third of the way down the container. In doing this try not to disturb any fine debris which may be on the surface of the mead. Fix the tubing by binding it to the outside of the jar with a short length of adhesive tape. This is important because with subsequent manipulations the tube may slip further into the jar and disturb the bottom sediment.

The reason for positioning the inlet of the tubing not more than a third of the way down the jar is to avoid any risk that a strong siphonic action might draw up deposit from the bottom of the container.

Place the tip of the outlet end of the tubing between the lips and gently suck to start the siphon. When the mead is running, pinch the tube firmly between the finger and thumb to stop the flow and wipe the end which has been in the mouth with a clean cloth. Keep this end well below the level of mead in the demijohn so as to maintain the siphon force, put it into the bottle, release the grip on the tubing, push the tubing down to the bottom of the bottle and allow the bottle to fill to a point about half an inch below the point which will be reached by the bottom of the cork. When bottling, it is desirable to push the tubing down to the bottom of the bottle so that the outlet is below the fluid level during the filling. This is to minimize splashing and frothing which has the deleterious effect of allowing oxygen into the mead.

Having filled the bottle to the correct level, allow it to stand for a few minutes so that any bubbles can rise to the surface and disperse. Then examine the bottle contents against a strong light to make sure there is no floating debris. If all is well the bottle should be polished with a soft cloth that has been moistened with methylated spirits. Give a final polish with a clean dry cloth and thereafter only handle the bottle in a clean cloth. Greasy finger prints on a bottle are most unattractive!

The final task is to label the bottle. Labels will be received from the show secretary. Check that they are for the correct class for your entry because mistakes do occur. The show schedule will usually contain instructions about the placement of the labels on bottles, or they may be enclosed with the labels. It is absolutely essential to meticulously follow these instructions. If the instruction is that 'the bottom of the label should be one inch from the bottom of the bottle' that is where it should be: not an inch and a half, or threequarters of an inch! Measure the exact distance with a ruler.

On most bottles two fine seams can be seen and felt running down opposite sides. When applying a label stand the bottle facing you with the seams to left and right so that the label can be affixed mid way between them. If it is an oblong label ensure that it is horizontal and not angulated. And keep it clean!

Presentation is important. Although immaculate presentation will not get a prize for bad mead it may well help a good mead into the winning position.

CHAPTER 11

JUDGING MEAD

It takes some years of experience to become a competent show judge of mead. The first requirement for the would-be mead judge is to acquire a broad understanding of the beverage by making it regularly. Success on the show bench at county and national levels should then be achieved, not an isolated first prize which might have been a 'fluke', but numerous high awards which will confirm consistent performance. After reaching this high standard as an exhibitor, the next step is to seek guidance and training in the techniques of judging by acting as a steward to acknowledged judges at major shows. When all these milestones in training have been passed it is then appropriate to start judging at local club level. As confidence and technique improve and your ability becomes recognized by colleagues, invitations to officiate at larger and more prestigious events should be forthcoming. I believe that this sequence of practical experience produces competent judges of mead. However, acknowledging that mead is a wine, albeit a unique one, an appropriate recognized qualification would be that of an amateur wine judge. Such qualifications are awarded by the National Guild of Wine and Beer Judges (Secretary - I.D.Allonby, 19 Manor Approach, Kimberworth, Rotherham, S61 IPZ) and the Wine and Spirit Education Trust, Five Kings House, 1 Queen Street Place, London, EC4R 1QS. It must be emphasized, however, that their examinations require a wide knowledge of wines and have very little focus on mead.

Judging Equipment
The following basic equipment is required for judging mead at a show.

The Show Schedule
Pens, paper, marking sheets, clip board
Spittoon and funnel
Glass cloth
At least six plain, colourless, clear glass tasting glasses of at least 4 oz capacity, with tulip shaped bowl
Corkscrew and spare corks
Palate refresher such as plain biscuits
Hydrometer and jar
Many larger shows expect judges to wear a white coat and hat
Bowls and water for washing glasses should be provided by the show officials.

Before judging
Always arrive in good time for the judges' briefing having studied the schedule carefully beforehand. If there are any doubts, settle these with the Show Secretary and/or the Judges Referee. Make sure your judging table is positioned in good light and instruct the steward on the way you wish to work. Check with the steward the location of all the bottles in the classes to be judged so that none will be overlooked.

At this stage it is appropriate to ascertain if there are duplicate entries in the classes. Most shows only allow an exhibitor to take one prize in a class so it is normal practice to judge the duplicate entries first allowing only the best example to go forward in the competition.

Indicate to the steward the order in which you wish to judge the classes. Always judge dry mead before sweet because it is impossible to do justice to a dry wine immediately after the palate has been exposed to sweet varieties.

Marking Sheet
To maintain a consistent judging standard it is important to work with a marking sheet. The National Guild of Wine and Beer Judges suggest that the Standard Marks for Still Wines should be as follows

Presentation	Clarity	Colour	Bouquet	Flavour & Balance	Total
2	4	4	10	30	50

That, of course, is highly reputable authoritative advice which can be followed with confidence. However, through personal experience I have come to prefer a slightly different allocation of marks, giving a little more weight to 'Flavour & Balance', and marking out of a hundred rather than fifty. My allocation of marks is, therefore, as follows.

Presentation	Clarity & Colour	Bouquet	Flavour, Balance, Body	Total
5	10	10	75	100

It would be arrogant and presumptuous of me to suggest that my allocation of marks is best. All I would claim is that it suits my approach to judging. Whatever marking system you adopt it is important to stick to it so as to achieve consistency in your deliberations.

A simple marking sheet, as used by the author, is illustrated in the Appendix.

Presentation

The bottle, cork and labels etc. must be as stipulated in the schedule. If they are not the judge can legitimately disqualify the entry.

Bottles, corks, and labels should be clean and of good quality. Marks should be deducted if they are not. Labels should be neatly applied in the position indicated in the schedule

Clarity & Colour

A good exhibit should be brilliantly clear. Mead of a dark yellow colour is always attractive but other colours are acceptable. Melomels etc. will, of course, vary with the colour of the fruit from which they were made.

When examining for clarity, bottles should not be inverted but kept upright and given a quick twist to disturb and bring into view sediment and particles. If these are present marks must be deducted.

An obviously cloudy wine would not be awarded any points and in my opinion should not progress further in the competition. A brilliant, particle-free exhibit, of good colour, should be awarded the full ten points.

With deeply coloured melomels, pyments etc., it may be difficult to judge clarity in the bottle. In those circumstances it is helpful to examine a sample in a glass.

Bouquet

The smell of a wine is its bouquet, sometimes known as its 'nose'. Occasionally, judges may be seen smelling the wine in the bottle as the cork is removed. In my view this is often a misleading practice and I am firmly of the opinion that bouquet should be assessed in the glass. To do this, fill the wine glass about a quarter full and then holding it by the lower part of the stem, swirl the mead around for a few seconds and then smell it carefully by placing the nose well into the top of the glass.

The bouquet should be clean and attractive with no unpleasant smells and sulphur dioxide should not be obvious. An aroma of honey should be detectable. The intensity of the bouquet is important, those with a pronounced aromatic attractive nose should be awarded more points than those with a weak bouquet.

Melomels, pyment, cyser, metheglin etc. will, of course, have a more pronounced bouquet than a plain mead. These wines should have a bouquet which is fruity and vinous with a hint of honey in the background.

A mead with a repulsive bouquet should not be awarded any points and, furthermore, should not progress further in the competition.

Flavour, Balance, Body

These characteristics are assessed by tasting. In tasting a wine it is important to take a reasonable quantity into the mouth and swill it around so as to bring it into contact with all parts of the tongue and also to encourage the aroma to pervade upwards into the area where the nasal airway comes into the upper back part of the mouth.. This is helpful because the senses of taste and smell are so closely inter-related.

The primary tastes of sweetness, acidity, bitterness and saltiness are detected in different areas of the tongue: sweetness at the front, acidity along the edge, bitterness at the back and saltiness along the front edges. Astringency due to excess tannin is felt as an uncomfortable drying sensation on the insides of the cheeks and along the gums and teeth.

The initial appreciation of sweetness is important to establish that the mead is in the correct class. A dry mead should have no detectable sweetness. If necessary this can be confirmed by resort to the hydrometer which should register a SG. of 1.000 or lower. Meads in the sweet class should be obviously sweet to the taste, but not sickly so. A SG somewhere in the range 1.010 to 1.020 is usually the most acceptable.

Sadly, many medium meads (around a SG of 1.005) get entered into dry classes. In a class designated for dry mead these must be disqualified as NAS (i.e. not according to schedule).

Mead should have sufficient acidity to give it a clean, refreshing taste. If insufficient acid is present the wine will be flabby and dull. There should also be tannin present to give a little astringency.

Alcohol content gives a warm feeling at the back of the throat. This should be of pleasant degree but if the sensation is excessive it is reasonable to suspect that the wine has been fortified. If that remains a strong suspicion the mead should not be awarded a prize.

Flavour is probably the most important quality of a wine. It is discerned by an interaction of the overall sensory stimulation by aroma on receptors at the back of the nose and the effect of the wine on taste buds on the tongue.

A wine is described as well balanced when its alcoholic strength, acidity, residual sugar, tannins etc. complement each other so that no single one of them dominates the palate. It is a quality that is distinct from flavour.

'Body' is the wine tasting term for the 'weight', i.e. the sensation of fullness resulting from the viscosity or density of a wine on the palate. Alcoholic strength and dissolved solids are the main factors which increase the body of a wine.

Finally, when it comes to swallowing, or spitting the wine into a spittoon, the time that the flavour of the mead persists in the mouth should be noted. This in tasting terminology is known as 'length'. The longer the flavour persists the better. Furthermore, when the flavour of the wine has disappeared the mouth should be left pleasantly fresh with no hint of any disagreeable after taste.

The quality of a mead is really a judgement made on a summation of all the desirable characteristics which have been mentioned. A high quality mead should be an excellent example of its kind and not just an ordinary passable beverage.

When all these characteristics have been assessed a mark is recorded.

Clearly, the assessment of bouquet, flavour, balance and quality are all dependent on the nose and palate of the individual judge. The sensitivity and responses of the noses and palates of different judges vary. This explains why an exhibit may be placed first in one show and perhaps second or third in another. Judges and exhibitors should not be disheartened by such occurrences.

When all the exhibits have been judged, marks allocated and totted-up, the order of merit should be clear but if there is a tie, the exhibits concerned must be looked at again and a decision made. Sometimes all the exhibits in a class are of poor quality and it is then necessary to consult with the Show Secretary about awards. At small local club shows it is customary to be generous and give prizes as an encouragement, but at county or national level an exhibit must be of high standard to receive a first prize..

Whenever possible the judge should stay for a time after a show opens and make himself, or herself, available to answer questions from exhibitors and public. This has educational and goodwill value.

GLOSSARY

Acetification   The oxidation of alcohol to acetic acid caused by infection of wine by acetobacter bacteria.

Acid   The main acids in fruits used for wine making are malic, citric and tartaric.

Aerobic, Anaerobic   Aerobic fermentation occurs in the presence of oxygen: anaerobic fermentation is without oxygen.

Airlock   Glass or plastic device holding a water trap which prevents air entering a vessel whilst allowing carbon dioxide produced in fermentation to escape.

Aroma or Bouquet   The smell arising from a wine.

Astringency   The unpleasant dryness in the mouth produced by excess tannin.

Body   Tasting term to describe the sensation of 'weight' or density of a wine in the mouth.

Campden Tablets   Tablets of sodium metabisulphite which in acid solution liberate sulphur dioxide, a strong sterilizing agent.

Carbon dioxide   The gas given off during fermentation when sugar is converted into alcohol.

Cyser   Beverage made from the fermentation of honey and apple juice.

Demijohn   A one gallon glass jar used in winemaking.

Fermentation   The breakdown of sugars by yeasts into alcohol with the liberation of carbon dioxide.

Hippocras   A wine made from honey and grape juice to which herbs are added.

Hydrometer   An instrument used for measuring the Specific Gravity (density) of a fluid. In winemaking, if the Specific Gravity is known, the sugar content of a must or wine can be determined by reference to a table.

Lactic acid Lactic acid can be produced in wine by lactic bacteria from traces of sugar and malic acid.

Lees The sediment that collects at the bottom of a fermentation vessel, consisting of dead yeast cells, tartrates and other insoluble material.

Malic acid Acid found in apples, grapes and many fruits in varying quantity.

Malolactic fermentation Conversion of stronger malic acid in wine by lactic bacteria to weaker lactic acid and carbon dioxide. This is sometimes referred to as a secondary fermentation.

Melomel Wine made from honey and fruit juice, other than apple or grape.

Metheglin Mead to which spices are added.

Must The honey and water mixture before fermentation is complete.

Oxidation Wine and mead exposed to air will take up oxygen. This causes loss of flavour and browning of the wine.

Pyment Wine made from grape juice and honey.

Rack The process of removing clear wine from its sediment. Often done with a siphon

Sorbate Potassium sorbate inhibits the growth of yeast. It can be used to stop sweet wines re-starting fermentation after bottling.

Specific Gravity The weight or density of a solution as compared with an equal volume of water. Sugar contained in a liquid will increase the Specific gravity: alcohol reduces it.

Stuck Fermentation A fermentation that stops prematurely, often caused by excess sugar.

Tannin Chemical found in the bark of some trees and in the skins, seeds and stalks of fruit. Its astringent property, in appropriate amount, gives character and 'bite' to a wine.

Yeast Single celled micro-organism, of which

there are many species. The one used in wine making is *Saccharomyces cerevisiae.*

Yeast nutrient   Ammonium sulphate and ammonium phospate salts which provide nitrogen for yeast growth.

USEFUL ADDRESSES

Equipment suppliers:-

Spencer Homebrews, 410 Rayners Lane, Pinner, Middlesex HA5
Most Branches of Boots the Chemists.

National Honey Show:-

Currently late November in Kensington Town Hall.
Hon. Secretary: Revd. F. Capener, 1 Baldric Road, Folkestone CT20 2NR (Publications include a useful leaflet on mead)

Labels etc:-

E. H. Thorne Ltd., Beehive Works, Wragby, Lincolnshire LN3 5LA
EBS, Okehampton, Devon, EX20 IUD
Steele & Brodie, Wormit, Fife, Scotland, DD6 8PG

Books:-

BBNO, 10 Quay Road, Charlestown, Cornwall, PL25 3NX
NBB, Scout Bottom Farm, Mytholmroyd, Hebden Bridge, Yorks, HX7 5JS.

APPENDIX

Conversion tables.

Temperature

°C	0	4	8	12	16	20	24	28	32	36
°F	32	39	46	54	61	68	75	82	90	97

Weight

1 oz	=	28 grams (g)	1000 milligrams	=	1 gram
1 lb	=	0.45 kilograms (kg)	1000 grams	=	1 kilogram
2.2 lbs	=	1 kilogram			

Volume

1 pint	=	0.568 litres
1.76 pints	=	1 litre
1 gallon	=	4.5 litres
1 litre	=	1000 millilitres

MARKING SHEET

Class Number			Description			
Exhibit No.	Presentation Bottle, Cork Label 5%	Clarity Colour 10%	Bouquet 10%	Flavour Balance Body 75%	Total 100%	Remarks

INDEX

A Collecti< Vintage Knitting Patterns for the Making of Summer Cardigans for Women

British Library Cataloguing-in-Publication Data
A catalogue record for this book is available from the
British Library

Dressmaking and Tailoring

Dressmaking and Tailoring broadly refers to those who make, repair or alter clothing for a profession. A dressmaker will traditionally make custom clothing for women, ranging from dresses and blouses to full evening gowns (also historically called a mantua-maker or a modiste). Whereas a tailor will do the same, but usually for men's clothing - especially suits. The terms essentially refer to a specific set of hand and machine sewing skills, as well as pressing techniques that are unique to the construction of traditional clothing. This is separate to 'made to measure', which uses a set of pre-existing patterns. Usually, a bespoke tailored suit or dress will be completely original and unique to the customer, and hence such items have been highly desirable since the trade first appeared in the thirteenth century. The Oxford English Dictionary states that the word 'tailor' first came into usage around the 1290s, and undoubtedly by this point, tailoring guilds, as well as those of cloth merchants and weavers were well established across Europe.

As the tailoring profession has evolved, so too have the methods of tailoring. There are a number of distinctive business models which modern tailors may practice, such as 'local tailoring' where the tailor is met locally, and the garment is produced locally too, 'distance tailoring', where a garment is ordered from an out-of-town tailor, enabling cheaper labour to be used -

which, in practice can now be done on a global scale via e-commerce websites, and a 'travelling tailor', where the man or woman will travel between cities, usually stationing in a luxury hotel to provide the client the same tailoring services they would provide in their local store. These processes are the same for both women's and men's garment making.

Pattern making is a very important part of this profession; the construction of a paper or cardboard template from which the parts of a garment are traced onto fabric before cutting our and assembling. A custom dressmaker (or tailor) frequently employs one of three pattern creation methods; a 'flat-pattern method' which begins with the creation of a sloper or block (a basic pattern for a garment, made to the wearer's measurements), which can then be used to create patterns for many styles of garments, with varying necklines, sleeves, dart placements and so on. Although it is also used for womenswear, the 'drafting method' is more commonly employed in menswear and involves drafting a pattern directly onto pattern paper using a variety of straightedges and curves. Since menswear rarely involves draping, pattern-making is the primary preparation for creating a cut-and-sew woven garment. The third method, the 'pattern draping method' is used when the patternmaker's skill is not matched with the difficulty of the design. It involves creating a muslin mock-up pattern, by pinning fabric directly on a dress form, then transferring the muslin outline and markings onto a paper pattern or using the muslin as the pattern itself.

Dressmaking and tailoring has become a very well respected profession; dressmakers such as Pierre Balmain, Christian Dior, Cristóbal Balenciaga and Coco Chanel have gone on to achieve international acclaim and fashion notoriety. Balmain, known for sophistication and elegance, once said that 'dressmaking is the architecture of movement.' Whilst tailors, due to the nature of their profession - catering to men's fashions, have not garnered such levels of individual fame, areas such as 'Savile Row' in the United Kingdom are today seen as the heart of the trade.

Knitting

Knitting is a method by which thread or yarn is used to create a cloth. This knitted fabric will always consist of consecutive rows of loops, called stitches. As each row progresses, the knitter will pull a new loop through an existing loop, with the active stiches held on a needle – until another loop can be passed through them. Knitting can be done by hand or machine, though most commonly it is a skilled craft created by hand – originally by country people with easy access to fibre. The word is derived from *knot* and ultimately from the Old English *cnyttan*, to knot. One of the earliest known examples of true knitting was cotton socks with stranded knit color patterns found in Egypt from the end of the first millennium AD. Initially a male-only occupation, the first knitting trade guild was started in Paris in 1527.

The process of knitting has three basic tasks:

1. The active (unsecured) stitches must be held so they don't drop.
2. These stitches must be released sometime after they are secured.
3. New bights of yarn must be passed through the fabric, usually through active stitches, thus securing them.

In very simple cases, knitting can be done without tools, using only the fingers to do these tasks; however, knitting is usually carried out using tools such as knitting needles, knitting machines or rigid frames. There are three basic types of knitting needles (also called 'knitting pins'). The first and most common type consists of two slender, straight sticks tapered to a point at one end, and with a knob at the other end to prevent stitches from slipping off. Such needles are usually 10–16 inches (250–410 mm) long but, due to the compressibility of knitted fabrics, may be used to knit pieces significantly wider. The most important property of needles is their diameter, which ranges from below 2 to 25 mm (roughly 1 inch). The diameter affects the size of stitches, which affects the gauge/tension of the knitting and the elasticity of the fabric. The yarn to be knitted is usually sold as balls or skeins, labelled as to its weight, length, dye lot, washing instructions – and suggested needle size. It is common practice amongst many knitters to keep these labels, for future reference if finishing / mending pieces.

Different types of yarns and needles may be used to achieve a plethora of knitted materials; these tools give the final piece a different colour, texture, weight, and/or integrity. Other factors that affect the end result include the needle's shape, thickness and malleability, as well as the yarn's fibre type, texture and twist. There are two major varieties of knitting: 'weft knitting' and 'warp knitting.' In the more common *weft knitting*, the wales (a sequence of stitches in which each stitch is suspended from the next) are perpendicular to the course of the yarn. In *warp knitting*, the wales and courses run roughly parallel, thus making them resistant to runs (commonly used in lingerie). In weft knitting, the entire fabric may be produced from a single yarn, by adding stitches to each wale in turn. By contrast, in warp knitting, one yarn is required for every wale. Since a typical piece of knitted fabric may have hundreds of wales, warp knitting is typically done by machine, whereas weft knitting is done by both hand and machine.

There are two further, important subdivisions in knitting: 'knit' and 'purl' stitches. In securing the previous stitch in a wale, the next stitch can pass through the previous loop from either below or above. If the former, the stitch is denoted as a *knit stitch* or a *plain stitch*; if the latter, as a *purl stitch*. The two stitches are related in that a knit stitch seen from one side of the fabric appears as a purl stitch on the other side. The two types of stitches have a different visual effect; the knit stitches look like 'V's stacked vertically, whereas the purl stitches look like a wavy horizontal line across the fabric. Patterns and pictures can be created in knitted fabrics by using knit and purl stitches as 'pixels'; however, such pixels are usually rectangular, rather than square, depending on the gauge/tension of the knitting. Individual stitches, or rows of stitches, may be made taller by drawing more yarn into the new loop (an elongated stitch), which is the basis for uneven knitting: a row of tall stitches may alternate with one or more rows of short stitches for an interesting visual effect.

Depending on the yarn and knitting pattern, knitted garments can stretch as much as 500%. For this reason, knitting was initially developed for garments that must be elastic or stretch in response to the wearer's motions, such as socks and hosiery. However, if they are not secured, the loops of a knitted course will come undone when their yarn is pulled; this is known as *ripping out, unravelling* knitting, or humorously, *frogging* (because you 'rip it', this sounds like a frog croaking: 'rib-bit'). To secure a stitch, at least one new loop is passed through it. Although the new stitch is itself unsecured ('active' or 'live'), it secures the stitch(es) suspended from it. To secure the initial stitches of a knitted fabric, a method for casting on is used; to secure the final stitches in a wale, one uses a method of binding/casting off. During knitting, the active stitches are secured mechanically, either from individual hooks (in knitting machines) or from a knitting needle or frame in hand-knitting.

Hand-knitting has gone into and out of fashion many times in the last two centuries, and at the turn of the twenty-first century it is now enjoying a revival. According to the industry group 'Craft Yarn Council of America', the number of women knitters in the United States age 25–35 increased 150% in the two years between 2002 and 2004. The latest incarnation is less about the 'make-do and mend' attitude of the 1940s and early 50s and more about making a statement about individuality as well as developing an innate sense of community. Additionally, many contemporary knitters have an interest in blogging about their knitting, patterns, and techniques, or joining a virtual community focused on knitting, such as the extremely popular 'Ravelry'. There are also a number of popular knitting podcasts, and various other knitting websites and knitting circles to join. We hope that the reader enjoys this book, and is encouraged to start some knitting of their own.

Contents

Attractive buttoned cardi-gan-sweater is sensible fash-ion for holidays, and this lively design looks very gay and striking in a sparkling pink,

Measurements: To fit 34–36 inch bust; length from top of shoulders, 23 ins.; sleeve seam, 16½ ins.

Tension: Equivalent to a basic tension of 5½ sts. and 7½ rows to an inch over stocking-stitch on No. 8 needles.

Abbreviations: *M.1P.*—Make 1 by picking up horizontal loop lying before next stitch and purling into back of it. *M.1K.*—Make 1 by pick-ing up horizontal loop lying before next stitch and knitting into back of it.

Materials: 20 ozs. Patons Double Quick Knitting in Strawberry Ice 243. A pair each No. 10 and No. 8 "Queen Bee" needles. 7 buttons.

BACK
With No. 10 needles, cast on 105 sts. and work 7 rows stocking-stitch, starting with a knit row. NEXT ROW: p. 3, * p. 3, p. twice in next st.; rep. from * to last 6 sts., p. 6: 129 sts.

1

Pineapple Stitch Cardigan

Change to No. 8 needles and Pineapple stitch. 1ST ROW: right side facing, * p. 2, k. 5, p. 1; rep. from * to last st., p. 1. 2ND ROW: * k. 2, p. 5, k. 1; rep. from * to last stitch, k. 1.
3RD ROW: * k. 1, p. 1, M.1 P., slip 1, k. 1, pass slipped stitch over, k. 1, k. 2 tog., M.1 P., p. 1; rep. from * to last stitch, k. 1. 4TH ROW: * p. 1, k. 2, p. 3, k. 2; rep. from * to last stitch, p. 1.
5TH ROW: * k. 1, M.1 K., p. 2, sl. 1, k. 2 tog., p.s.s.o., p. 2, M.1 K.; rep. from * to last st., k. 1. 6TH ROW: * p. 2, k. 2, p. 1, k. 2, p. 1; rep. from * to last st., p. 1. 7TH ROW: * k. 1, M.1 K., k. 1, p. 2 tog., p. 1, p. 2 tog., k. 1, M.1 K.; rep. from * to last st., k. 1.
8TH ROW: * p. 3, k. 3, p. 2; rep. from * to last st., p. 1. 9TH ROW: * k. 1, k. 2 tog., M.1 P., p. 1, k. 1, p. 1, M.1 P., sl. 1, k. 1, p.s.s.o.; rep. from * to last st., k. 1. 10TH ROW: as 6th.
11TH ROW: k. 2 tog., * p. 2, M.1 K., k. 1, M.1 K., p. 2, sl. 1, k. 2 tog., p.s.s.o.; rep. from * to last 7 sts., p. 2, M.1 K., k. 1, M.1 K., p. 2, sl. 1, k. 1, p.s.s.o. 12TH ROW: as 4th. 13TH ROW: * p. 1, p. 2 tog., k. 1, M.1 K., k. 1, M.1 K., k. 1, p. 2 tog.; rep. from * to last st., p. 1. 14TH ROW: as 2nd.
Rows 3–14 inclusive form pattern. Rep. them 4 times more, then rows 3–13 inclusive again. NEXT ROW: p. 1, (p. 2, p. 2 tog.) 3 times, (p. 3, p. 2 tog.) 20 times, (p. 2, p. 2 tog.) 3 times, p. 4; 103 sts.
Change to rib pattern. 1ST ROW: right side facing, * p. 1, k. 1; rep. from * to last 3 sts., p. 3. 2ND ROW: * k. 3, p. 1; rep. from * to last 3 sts., k. 3. These 2 rows form rib pattern. Continue straight in rib until back measures 15 ins. from start of Pineapple stitch, ending with right side facing.
Shape armholes by casting off 4 sts. at beg. of next 2 rows, then decrease 1 st. at each end of next and every alternate row until 79 sts. remain. Work straight until back measures 23 ins.
With right side facing, shape shoulders by casting off 8 sts. at beg. of next 6 rows. Cast off remaining 31 sts.

FRONTS

Left: With No. 10 needles, cast on 56 sts. and work 7 rows stocking-stitch, starting with a knit row. NEXT ROW: cast on 8, p. 8, * p. 3, p. twice in next st.; rep. from * to last 4 sts., p. 4; 77 sts.
Change to No. 8 needles and pattern as for back keeping 4 sts. at front edge in stocking-stitch throughout. Your first 4 rows will read:—1ST ROW: * p. 2, k. 5, p. 1; rep. from * to last 5 sts., p. 1, slip 1 purlways, k. 3. 2ND ROW: p. 4, * k. 2, p. 5, k. 1; rep. from * to last st., k. 1.
3RD ROW: * k. 1, p. 1, M.1 P., sl. 1, k. 1, p.s.s.o., k. 1, k. 2 tog., M.1 P., p. 1; rep. from * to last 5 sts., k. 1, slip 1 purlways, k. 3. 4TH ROW: p. 4, * p. 1, k. 2, p. 3, k. 2; rep. from * to last st., p. 1.
Continue in Pineapple stitch, slipping 4th st. in from front edge throughout on next and every alternate row until 13th row of 6th pattern has been worked to match back.
NEXT ROW: p. 12, (p. 2 tog., p. 2) twice, (p. 2 tog., p. 3) 9 times, (p. 2 tog., p. 2) 3 times: 63 sts.
Change to rib pattern. 1ST ROW: p. 3, k. 1; rep. from * to last 7 sts., p. 3, slip 1 purlways, k. 3. 2ND ROW: p. 4, * k. 3, p. 1; rep. from * to last 3 sts., k. 3. Rep. the last 2 rows until front matches back at side edge, ending with right side facing.
Shape armhole by casting off 4 sts. at beg. of next row, then decrease 1 st. at this edge on following 8 alternate rows: 51 sts. Continue straight until work measures 21 ins. ending with wrong side facing.
Shape neck by casting off 16 sts. at beg. of next row, then decrease 1 st. at this edge on every row until 24 sts. remain. Work a few rows straight until front matches back at armhole edge.
With right side facing, shape shoulder by casting off 8 sts. at beg. of next and following 2 alternate rows, armhole edge.
Right: With No. 10 needles, cast on 56 sts. and work 7 rows stocking-stitch, starting with a knit row. NEXT ROW: p. 4, * p. twice in next st., p. 3; rep. from * to end, turn and cast on 8: 77 sts.
With right side facing, change to No. 8 needles and work to correspond with left front with the addition of 7 buttonholes. First to come in 9th and 10th rows of 1st pattern; 2nd in 9th and 10th rows of 3rd pattern; 3rd in 9th and 10th rows of 5th pattern and remaining 4 spaced at equal intervals up to within 1-inch of start of neck shaping.
First mark position of buttons on left front with pins to ensure even spacing, then make buttonholes to correspond. To make a buttonhole:—right side facing, k. 3, sl. 1 purlways, pattern 3, cast off 3, pattern to end; pattern back casting on 3 over those cast off.

SLEEVES

With No. 10 needles, cast on 50 sts. and work 2¼ ins.
k. 1, p. 1 rib, increasing 1 st. at end of last row: 51 sts.

Change to No. 8 needles and rib pattern as follows:—
1ST ROW: * p. 3, k. 1; rep. from * to last 3 sts., p. 3. 2ND
ROW: * k. 3, p. 1; rep. from * to last 3 sts., k. 3. These
2 rows form rib pattern.

Continue in pattern, shaping sides by increasing 1 st. at
each end of next and every following 8th row until there
are 75 sts. Continue straight until sleeve seam measures
16½ ins.

With right side facing, shape top by casting off 4 sts. at
beg. of next 2 rows, then decrease 1 st. at each end of next
and every alternate row until 37 sts. remain. Pattern back,
then decrease 1 st. at each end of every row until 17 sts.
remain. Cast off.

COLLAR

With No. 10 needles, cast on 92 sts. 1ST ROW: p. 2,
* k. 1, p. 2; rep. from * to end. 2ND ROW: k. 2, * p. 1,
k. 2; rep. from * to end. Rep. these 2 rows 5 times more,
then 1st row again. NEXT ROW: p. 5, * p. twice in next st.,
p. 3; rep. from * to last 3 sts., p. 3: 113 sts.

Change to No. 8 needles and Pineapple stitch as given
for back and work rows 1–14 inclusive once, then rows
3–12 inclusive once. Cast off in pattern.

TO MAKE UP

Pin ribbed parts out to size and press lightly on wrong side
under a damp cloth. Join shoulder and side seams matching
pattern carefully. Join sleeve seams; insert sleeves. Turn under
stocking-stitch all round lower edge and slip-hem on wrong
side.

Turn under stocking-stitch up to the slipped stitch down
front edges and slip-hem on wrong side. Pin cast-on edge of
collar round neck, starting and ending ¾-inch in from front
edges. Sew in position. Press all seams and hems lightly. Sew
on buttons.

Bouclet gives

an attractive

casual fabric

close-up of man's
pullover only

WHITE DOLMAN BUTTON-UP

Materials: 10 (11) ozs. Patons Beehive Bouclet in White, and 3 (3) ozs. Patons Beehive Fingering 4-ply, Patonised, in White. A pair each No. 12 and No. 11 "Queen Bee" needles—the No. 11 needles to be 14 inch. Eleven buttons. Facing ribbon for front edges if required.

Measurements: To fit 35–36 (37–38) inch bust; length from top of shoulders, 20 (20) inches; sleeve seam, 17½ (17½) inches.

Tension: 7¼ sts. and 10 rows to an inch over stocking-stitch in Bouclet on No. 11 needles.

N.B.—Instructions for large size given in brackets thus ( ). Where one set of figures is given, this applies to both sizes.

BACK

With No. 12 needles and the 4-ply wool, cast on 111 (119) sts. and work 4 inches k. 1, p. 1 rib, rows on right side having a k. 1 at each end.

With right side facing, change to No. 11 needles and Bouclet wool, and continue in stocking-stitch, starting with a knit row, shaping sides by increasing 1 stitch at each end of 3rd and every following 6th row until there are 133 (141) sts. Work 3 rows straight.

With right side facing, shape for sleeves as follows:—Cast on 16 (16) sts. at beginning of next 4 rows, then 9 (9) sts. at beginning of next 16 rows: 341 (349) sts. Now work straight until cuff edge of sleeve measures 5 inches.

With right side facing, shape shoulders by casting off 11 (11) sts. at beginning of next 18 rows, then 6 (8) sts. at beginning of next 2 rows, then 6 (6) sts. at beginning of following 16 rows. Cast off remaining 35 (39) sts.

FRONTS

Left: With No. 12 needles and the 4-ply wool, cast on 53 (57) sts. and work 4 inches k. 1, p. 1 rib, rows on right side having a k. 1 at each end.

With right side facing, change to No. 11 needles and Bouclet wool and continue in stocking-stitch, shaping side edge by increasing 1 stitch at beginning of 3rd and every following 6th row until there are 64 (68) sts. Work 3 rows straight.

With right side facing, shape sleeve by casting on 16 (16) sts. at beginning of next and following alternate row, then 9 (9) sts. at beginning of following 8 alternate rows: 168 (172) sts. Work straight until cuff edge measures 5 inches.

With right side facing, start to shape shoulder by casting off 11 (11) sts. at beginning of next and following 4 alternate rows. Now, with wrong side facing, include neck shaping by casting off 7 (9) sts. at beginning of next row, then decrease 1 stitch at this edge on following 8 alternate rows, then keep this edge straight, and *at the same time* continue shaping shoulder as before by casting off 11 (11) sts. at beginning of next 4 knit rows, then 6 (8) sts. at beginning of following knit row, then 6 (6) sts. at beginning of following 8 knit rows.

Right: Work to correspond with left front reversing shapings.

TO MAKE UP

Press work lightly on wrong side under a damp cloth, avoiding ribbing. Join shoulder seams. *Cuffs:* With No. 12 needles, right side facing and 4-ply wool, pick up and k. 60 (60) sts. across each sleeve edge. Work 3 inches k. 1, p. 1 rib; cast off loosely in rib. Join side and underarm seams. *Borders:* With No. 12 needles and 4-ply wool, cast on 11 sts. and work a strip in k.1, p.1 rib to fit up left front when slightly stretched. Sew in position and leave stitches on a safety-pin at top.

Work a similar strip for right front with the addition of 10 buttonholes—first to come ¼ inch from lower edge, 10th about 1¼ inches from top, allowing for 11th hole in neckband later, and remaining 8 evenly spaced between. First mark position of buttons on left front with pins to ensure even spacing, then work holes to correspond. To make a buttonhole:—Rib 4, cast off 3, rib to end and back, casting on 3 over those cast off. Sew border in position and leave stitches on a pin at top; face borders with ribbon on wrong side if desired.

Neck: With No. 12 needles, 4-ply wool and right side facing, pick up and k. 109 (115) sts. all round neck including those on safety-pins. Work ½-inch k. 1, p. 1 rib, then make a buttonhole in next 2 rows; work 1 inch straight, then make another buttonhole in next 2 rows; work ½ inch straight, then cast off loosely, using a bigger needle. Fold neckband in half to wrong side and slip-hem; oversew round double buttonhole. Press seams. Sew on buttons.

5

A STITCH FOR LARGE SIZES

MATERIALS: Of Patons Beehive Fingering 2-ply, Patonised, 7 ozs. for short sleeves, 8 ozs. for long sleeves. A pair each No. 11 and No. 12 "Queen Bee" needles. Fourteen buttons.

MEASUREMENTS: To fit 40–42-inch bust; length from top of shoulders, 19½ inches; sleeve seam, 17½ and 5½ inches.

TENSION: 8 sts. to an inch.

N.B.—Bobble: Cast on 4 sts. to next stitch on left-hand needle, p. 5, slip 4th stitch over 5th, 3rd over 5th, 2nd over 5th, 1st over 5th, leave 5th stitch on right-hand needle.

BACK

With No. 12 needles cast on 118 sts. and work 3¼ inches k. 1, p. 1 rib. NEXT ROW: Knit, increasing to 131 sts. by working twice into every 9th stitch, 13 times. NEXT ROW: Purl.

Change to No. 11 needles and pattern. 1ST ROW: Right side facing, k. 8, * (bobble, k. 1) 3 times, k. 16; repeat from * ending last repeat, k. 7 instead of k. 16. 2ND AND ALTERNATE ROWS: Purl.

3RD ROW: k. 6, * (bobble, k. 1) 5 times, k. 12; repeat from * ending last repeat k. 5 instead of k. 12. 5TH ROW: k. 4, * bobble, k. 1, bobble, k. 7, bobble, k. 1, bobble, k. 9; repeat from * ending last repeat k. 4.

7TH ROW: k. 2, * bobble, k. 1, bobble, k. 11, bobble, k. 1, bobble, k. 5; repeat from * ending last repeat k. 2. 9TH ROW: k. 2, * bobble, k. 1, bobble, k. 5, bobble, k. 5, bobble, k. 1, bobble, k. 5; repeat from * ending last repeat k. 2.

Larger sizes can take a soft bobble pattern like this one. Without attempting to deliberately disguise the fuller figure, by adding an all-over interest the effect detracts from the more buxom lines.

11TH ROW: As 7th. 13TH ROW: As 5th. 15TH ROW: As 3rd. 17TH ROW: As 1st. 19TH ROW: k. 1, bobble, * k. 17, bobble, k. 1, bobble, k. 1, bobble; repeat from * ending last repeat k. 17, bobble, k. 1.

21ST ROW: (k. 1, bobble) twice, * k. 13, (bobble, k. 1) 4 times, bobble; repeat from * ending last repeat k. 13, (bobble, k. 1) twice. 23RD ROW: k. 3, bobble, k. 1, bobble, * k. 9, bobble, k. 1, bobble, k. 7, bobble, k.1, bobble; repeat from * ending last repeat k. 9, bobble, k. 1, bobble, k. 3.

25TH ROW: k. 5, bobble, k. 1, bobble, * k. 5, bobble, k. 1, bobble k. 11, bobble, k. 1, bobble; repeat from * ending last repeat k. 5, bobble, k. 1, bobble, k. 5. 27TH ROW: k. 5, bobble, k. 1, bobble, * k. 5, bobble, k. 1, bobble, k. 5, bobble, k. 5, bobble, k. 1, bobble; repeat from * ending last repeat k. 5, bobble, k. 1, bobble, k. 5.

29TH ROW: As 25th. 31ST ROW: As 23rd. 33RD ROW: As 21st.,

35TH ROW: As 19th. 36TH ROW: Purl. These 36 rows form pattern.

Continue in pattern, increasing 1 stitch at each end of next and every following 6th row, 4 times, taking extra sts. into stocking-stitch as they are made (139 sts.). Work straight until 2 complete patterns and 18 rows of 3rd have been done.

With right side facing, shape armholes thus:—NEXT ROW: Cast off 7, k. 16, bobble, k.1, bobble, k. 1, bobble; work 19th row from * to last 23 sts., k. 23. NEXT ROW: Cast off 7, purl to end. NEXT ROW: k. 2 tog., k. 12, (bobble, k. 1) 4 times, bobble; work 21st row from * to last 14 sts., k. 12, k. 2 tog. NEXT ROW: Purl.

NEXT ROW: k. 2 tog.; work 23rd row from * to last 11 sts., k.9, k. 2 tog. NEXT ROW: Purl. NEXT ROW: k. 2 tog., k. 1; work 25th row from * to last 8 sts., k. 6, k. 2 tog. NEXT ROW: purl. NEXT ROW: k. 2 tog.; work 27th row from * to last 7 sts., k. 5, k. 2 tog. NEXT ROW: Purl.

NEXT ROW: k. 2 tog., k. 4, bobble, k. 1, bobble, k. 11, bobble, k. 1, bobble; work 25th row from * to last 6 sts., k. 4, k. 2 tog. NEXT ROW: Purl. NEXT ROW: k. 2 tog., k. 5, bobble, k. 1, bobble, k. 7, bobble, k. 1, bobble; work 23rd row from * to last 7 sts., k.5, k.2 tog. NEXT ROW: Purl.

NEXT ROW: k. 2 tog., k. 6, (bobble, k. 1) 4 times, bobble; work 21st row from * to last 8 sts., k. 6, k. 2 tog. NEXT ROW: Purl. NEXT ROW: k. 2 tog., k. 7, bobble, k. 1, bobble, k. 1, bobble; work 19th row from * to last 9 sts., k. 7, k. 2 tog. NEXT ROW: Purl. (This completes armhole shaping and 109 sts. remain.)

Continue straight in pattern (as you have decreased half a pattern up armhole you can start again with the 19th row exactly as given) until 8 lines of bobbles have been done from start. Work 4 rows straight in stocking-stitch.

With right side facing, shape shoulders by casting off 11 sts. at beginning of next 6 rows; cast off remainder.

FRONTS

Left: With No. 12 needles cast on 62 sts. and work 3½ inches k. 1, p. 1 rib. NEXT ROW: knit, increasing 3 sts. evenly across (65 sts.). NEXT ROW: Purl.

Change to No. 11 needles and work 1 pattern straight, then continue in pattern, increasing 1 stitch at beginning of next and every following 6th row, side edge, 4 times, keeping extra sts. in stocking-stitch (69 sts.). Work straight until 2 complete patterns and 18 rows of 3rd are done.

With right side facing, shape armhole by casting off 7 sts. at beginning of next row, then k. 2 tog. at this edge on alternate rows, 9 times (33 sts. remain and last row of 4th pattern has been done). Work 4 rows straight in stocking-stitch.

With wrong side facing, shape neck:—Cast off 12 sts. at beginning of next row, then decrease 1 stitch at neck edge on alternate rows, 9 times (33 sts. remain and last row of 4th pattern has been done). Work 4 rows straight in stocking-stitch.

With right side facing, shape shoulder by casting off 11 sts. at beginning of next and following 2 alternate rows, armhole edge.

Right: Work to correspond with left, reversing shapings.

SLEEVES

Long: With No. 12 needles cast on 62 sts. and work 3 inches k. 1. NEXT ROW: Knit, increasing 3 sts. evenly across (65 sts.). NEXT ROW: Purl.

Change to No. 11 needles and pattern as for back, increasing 1 stitch at each end of 7th and every following 6th row until there are 87 sts., taking extra sts. into pattern as they are made. Continue in pattern, still increasing as before, but keeping extra sts. in stocking-stitch until there are 95 sts. Work straight until 3½ patterns have been done.

With right side facing, shape top by casting off 4 sts. at beginning of next 2 rows, then k. 2 tog. at beginning of every row until 49 sts. remain, then at each end of every row until 23 remain. Cast off.

Short: With No. 12 needles cast on 86 sts. and work 1½ inches k. 1, p. 1 rib. NEXT ROW: knit, increasing 1 stitch at end of row (87 sts.). NEXT ROW: purl.

Change to No. 11 needles and pattern, increasing 1 stitch at each end of 7th and every following 6th row, 4 times, taking extra sts. into stocking-stitch as they are made. Work straight to end of 1st pattern.

Shape top as for long sleeves.

RIBBED BANDS

Fronts: Join shoulder seams. With No. 12 needles cast on 15 sts. and work in k. 1, p. 1 rib, rows on right side having a k.1 at each end, until strip is long enough to go up left front when slightly stretched. Sew in position as you go along and leave sts. on a safety-pin at top.

Make a similar strip for right front with the addition of 13 buttonholes:—14th comes in neckband later. First comes ½-inch from bottom edge, 13th about ¼-inch from top and remainder at equal intervals. Mark position of buttons on left front with pins, then work holes to correspond. To make a buttonhole:—rib 6, cast off 3, rib 6, turn; rib 6, cast on 3, rib 6.

Neckband: With right side facing and No. 12 needles, rib 15 sts. from right front band, pick up and k. 85 sts. all round neck and rib remaining 15 from left front band. Work 1¼ inches rib, making 14th buttonhole after ½-inch has been done. Cast off.

TO MAKE UP

Do not press. Join side and sleeve seams; insert sleeves. Sew on buttons. Press seams.

7

Summer Outlook

CHART A

16 PATTERN STS

CHART B

16 PATTERN STS

KEY
☐ PINK ◉ GREEN

Pink is this summer's colour, and it looks so pretty against a soft deep green shade. Clever colour motif links the colour change to make a very flattering and feminine sweater to wear through the summer.

*　　*　　*

Materials: Of Patons Beehive Fingering, 4-ply, Patonised, 3/3/3 ozs. Woodland Green 1171 and 9/10/10 ozs. Pale Pink 245. A pair each No. 10 and No. 12 "Queen Bee" needles. 9 buttons.

Measurements: To fit 34–35/36–37/38–39 inch bust; length from top of shoulders, 22½/22½/23 ins.; sleeve seam, 16½ ins. all sizes.

Tension: 7 sts. and 9 rows to an inch over stocking-stitch on No. 10 needles.

N.B.—Instructions are given for 3 sizes. P.=Pale Pink. G.=Woodland Green.

BACK

With P. wool and No. 12 needles, cast on 130/138/146 sts. and work 16 rows k. 2, p. 2 rib, rows on right side having a k. 2 at each end.

With right side facing, change to No. 10 needles and stocking-stitch, starting with a knit row, and work straight until back measures 14¼ ins.

With right side facing, shape armholes by casting off 4 sts. at beg. of next 2 rows, then k. 2 tog. at each end of next and every alternate row until 102/108/112 sts. remain. Work straight until back measures 22½/22½/23 ins.

With right side facing, shape shoulders by casting off 10/10/11 sts. at beg. of next 2 rows, then 10/11/11 sts. at beg. of next 4 rows. Leave remaining 42/44/46 sts. on a spare needle.

8

Summer Outlook
Button-up Design

FRONTS

Left: With No. 12 needles, cast on 28 sts. in G. and 42/46/50 sts. in P. 1ST ROW: right side facing, k. 2 P., (p. 2, k. 2) 10/11/12 times in P., (p. 2, k. 2) 7/7/7 times in G. 2ND ROW: (p. 2, k. 2) 7/7/7 times in G., (p. 2, k. 2) 10/11/12 times in P., p. 2 P. Rep. the last 2 rows 7 times more twisting wools on wrong side of work when changing colour to avoid a hole.

With right side facing, change to No. 10 needles. NEXT ROW: k. 42/46/50 P., k. 28 G. NEXT ROW: cast on 9 in G. for facing, p. 37 G., p. 42/46/50 P.: 79/83/87 sts.

Continue in pattern introducing leaf motif from chart A. as follows:— 1ST ROW: k. 34/38/42 P., k. 16 as on 1st row of chart A., k. 20 G., slip 1 purlways, k. 8 G. 2ND ROW: p. 29 G., p. 16 as on 2nd row of chart A., p. 34/38/42 P.

Continue in pattern thus, working the pattern stitches from chart and repeating the 10 pattern rows throughout, reading odd rows knit from right to left and even rows purl from left to right, *at the same time* slipping the 9th stitch in from front edge on knit rows throughout.

Work straight in pattern until front matches back at side edge. With right side facing, continue in pattern shaping armhole by casting off 4 sts. at beg. of next row, then decrease 1 st. at armhole edge on following 10/11/13 alternate rows: 65/68/70 sts.

Continue straight in pattern until front measures 20½/20½/21 ins. With wrong side facing, shape neck as follows:— NEXT ROW: cast off 9, p. 14 and slip these stitches on a spare needle, p. 2 tog., work to end. Continue decreasing 1 st. at neck edge on every row until 30/32/33 sts. remain. Continue straight for a few rows until front matches back at armhole edge.

With right side facing, shape shoulder by casting off 10/10/11 sts. at beg. of next row, then 10/11/11 sts. at beg. of following 2 alternate rows, armhole edge.

Right: With No. 12 needles, cast on 42/46/50 sts. in P. and 28 sts. in G. 1ST ROW: (k. 2, p. 2) 7/7/7 times in G., (k. 2, p. 2) 10/11/12 times in P., k. 2 P. 2ND ROW: p. 2 P., (k. 2, p. 2) 10/11/12 times in P., (k. 2, p. 2) 7/7/7 times in G. Rep. the 1st and 2nd rows twice more. 7TH ROW: rib 3, cast off 3, rib to end. 8TH ROW: rib back casting on 3 over those cast off. Rep. 1st and 2nd rows 4 times more.

With right side facing, change to No. 10 needles. NEXT ROW: cast on 9 in G. for facing, k. 8, slip 1 purlways, k. 28 G., k. 42/46/50 P. NEXT ROW: p. 42/46/50 P., p. 37 G.

Introduce leaf motif from chart B. as follows:— 1ST ROW: k. 8, slip 1 purlways, k. 20 G., k. 16 as on 1st row of chart B., k. 34/38/42 P. 2ND ROW: p. 34/38/42 P., p. 16 as on 2nd row of chart B., p. 29 G.

Continue in pattern thus and work to correspond with left front with the addition of 7 more buttonholes. Place

8th buttonhole 2¼ ins. below start of neck shaping (this allows for 9th one in neckband) and remaining 6 spaced at about 2¼-inch intervals from 1st buttonhole in welt.

First mark position of buttons on left front with pins to ensure even spacing, then work holes to correspond. To make a double buttonhole:— right side facing, k. 3, cast off 3, k. 2, slip 1 purlways, k. 2, cast off 3, k. to end in pattern; purl back in pattern casting on 3 over those cast off.

SLEEVES

With No. 12 needles and P. wool, cast on 56/56/60 sts. and work 2½ ins. k. 2, p. 2 rib, increasing 1 st. at each end of last row: 58/58/62 sts.

With right side facing, change to No. 10 needles and stocking-stitch, starting with a knit row, and shape sides by increasing 1 st. at each end of 5th and every following 8th row until there are 86/86/90 sts. Work straight until sleeve seam measures 16½ ins.

With right side facing, shape top by casting off 4 sts. at beg. of next 2 rows, then k. 2 tog. at each end of next and every alternate row until 40/40/40 sts. remain. Now decrease 1 st. at each end of every row until 26/26/26 sts. remain. Cast off.

TO MAKE UP

Press parts lightly on wrong side under a damp cloth, avoiding ribbing.

Join shoulder, side and sleeve seams; insert sleeves. Fold under 8 sts. up to the slipped stitch down front edges and slip-hem lightly in position. Oversew loosely round double buttonholes.

Neckband: With No. 12 needles, G. wool and right side facing, k. 14/14/14 sts. from spare needle increasing 2 sts. evenly, pick up and k. 18/18/18 sts. up side of neck, join in P. and k. 42/44/46 from back increasing 4/6/4 sts. evenly, join in 2nd ball G. and pick up and k. 18/18/18 sts. down side of neck, then k. 14/14/14 from spare needle increasing 2 sts. evenly: 114/118/118 sts.

NEXT ROW: (p. 2, k. 2) 8/8/8 times in G., p. 2 G., (k. 2, p. 2) 11/12/12 times in P., k. 2 P., p. 2 G., (k. 2, p. 2) 8/8/8 times in G. Twist wools on wrong side of work when changing colour to avoid a hole.

Work a further 2 rows in rib. NEXT ROW: rib 3, cast off 3, rib to end. NEXT ROW: in rib, casting on 3 over those cast off. Work a further 6 rows in rib, then make a buttonhole in next 2 rows as before. Work 4 rows in rib. Cast off loosely in rib using the appropriate colours and a bigger needle.

Fold neckband in half to wrong side and slip-hem in position; oversew loosely round buttonhole. Press all seams. Sew on buttons.

9

lively designs from Vienna
bring a popular fashion
feature this month
making use of chunky
rib panels and a colour theme

Materials: 18 (19) ozs. Patons Double Quick Knitting in White. A pair each No. 8, No. 9 and No. 10 "Queen Bee" needles. Cable needle. 10 buttons. 1 press fastener.

Measurements: To fit 34–35 (36–37) inch bust; length from top of shoulders, 20½ (20¾) ins.; sleeve seam, 16 (16½) ins.

Tension: Equivalent to a basic tension of 5½ sts. and 7½ rows to an inch over stocking-stitch on No. 8 needles.

N.B.—Instructions for large size given in brackets thus ( ). Where one set of figures is given this applies to both sizes. Figures in square brackets also apply to both sizes.

11

CABLE CARDIGAN

CENTRE BACK PANEL

With No. 9 needles, cast on 52 (52) sts. and work in pattern thus:—1ST ROW: right side facing, p. 3, k. 6, [p. 2, k. 2] 8 (8) times, p. 2, k. 6, p. 3. 2ND ROW: k. 3, p. 6, [k. 2, p. 2] 8 (8) times, k. 2, p. 6, k. 3.

3RD ROW: p. 3, slip next 3 sts. on cable needle and leave at front of work, k. 3, k. 3 from cable needle, this will be called "cable 6", [p. 2, k. 2] 8 (8) times, p. 2, cable 6, p.3. 4TH ROW: As 2nd.

5TH–10TH ROWS: As 1st–2nd rows, 3 times. These 10 rows form pattern.

Change to No. 8 needles. Continue in pattern and with right side facing, start shaping panel as follows:—NEXT ROW: p. 3, k. 6, p. 2, [p. 1, k. 1] in next stitch, rib to last 12 sts., [k. 1, p. 1] in next stitch, p. 2, k. 6, p. 3. NEXT ROW: k. 3, p. 6, k. 3, rib to last 12 sts., k. 3, p. 6, k. 3. Work 6 rows straight in pattern, keeping the extra stitches in reversed stocking-stitch.

NEXT ROW: p. 3, k. 6, p. 2, increase in next stitch, rib to last 12 sts., increase in next stitch, p. 2, k. 6, p. 3. NEXT ROW: k. 3, p. 6, k. 4, rib to last 13 sts., k. 4, p. 6, k. 3. Work 6 rows straight in pattern, keeping extra stitches in reversed stocking-stitch.

NEXT ROW: p. 3, k. 6, p. 2, [k. 1, p. 1] in next stitch, p. 1, rib to last 12 sts., [p. 1, k. 1] in next stitch, p. 2, k. 6, p. 3. NEXT ROW: k. 3, p. 6, k. 2, p. 1, rib to last 12 sts., p. 1, k. 2, p. 6, k. 3. Work 6 rows straight in pattern, keeping continuity of the rib pattern. NEXT ROW: Pattern 11, increase in next stitch, rib to last 12 sts., increase in next stitch, pattern 11. Work 7 rows straight, keeping continuity of rib.

Continue thus, increasing 1 stitch inside the 11 border stitches at each end of next and every following 8th row until there are 64 (64) sts., taking extra stitches into rib pattern as before. Now increase 1 stitch as before at each end of rib on every following 6th row until there are 92 (92) sts. Work 11 (11) rows straight.

With right side facing, shape shoulders by casting off 9 (9) sts. at beginning of next 2 rows, then 8 (8) sts. at beginning of next 4 rows; leave remaining stitches on a spare needle.

LEFT FRONT PANEL

With No. 9 needles, cast on 24 (24) sts. 1ST ROW: right side facing, p. 3, k. 6, [p. 2, k. 2] 3 (3) times, p. 3. 2ND ROW: k. 3, [p. 2, k. 2] 3 (3) times, p. 6, k. 3.

3RD ROW: p. 3, cable 6, [p. 2, k. 2] 3 (3) times, p. 3. 4TH ROW: As 2nd. 5TH–10TH ROWS: As 1st–2nd rows, 3 times. These 10 rows form pattern for left front.

Change to No. 8 needles and with right side facing, continue in pattern and start increasing in rib pattern thus:—NEXT ROW: p. 3, k. 6, p. 2, [p. 1, k. 1] in next stitch, rib to last stitch, p. 1. NEXT ROW: k. 3, [p. 2, k. 2] 3 (3) times, k. 1, p. 6, k. 3. Work 6 rows straight in pattern, keeping extra stitches in reversed stocking-stitch.

Continue thus, increasing 1 stitch inside the 11 border stitches at beginning of next and every following 8th row until there are 30 (30) sts., then on every following 6th row until there are 44 (44) sts., keeping rib pattern as before. Work 11 (11) rows straight.

With right side facing, shape shoulder and neck edge thus:—Next 2 rows: Cast off 9, pattern to last 7 sts.; turn and pattern back. NEXT 2 ROWS: Cast off 8, pattern to last 13 sts.; turn and pattern back. NEXT ROW: Cast off 8; leave remaining 19 (19) sts. on a spare needle.

RIGHT FRONT PANEL

With No. 9 needles cast on 24 (24) sts. 1ST ROW: right side facing, p. 3, [k. 2, p. 2] 3 (3) times, k. 6, p. 3. 2ND ROW: k. 3, p. 6, [k. 2, p. 2] 3 (3) times, k. 3. 3RD ROW: p. 3, [k. 2, p. 2] 3 (3) times, cable 6, p. 3. 4TH ROW: As 2nd. 5TH–10TH ROWS: As 1st–2nd rows, 3 times.

Change to No. 8 needles and with right side facing, start increasing thus:—NEXT ROW: p. 3, [k. 2, p. 2] 2 (2) times, k. 1, [k. 1, p. 1] in next stitch, p. 2, k. 6, p. 3. Work 7 rows straight.

Finish to correspond with left front, reversing all shapings. Remember you will have wrong side instead of right side facing when doing shoulder and neck shaping.

BACK HALF OF RIGHT SLEEVE AND BACK PANEL

Join shoulder seams. With No. 10 needles, cast on 26 (26) sts. and work 2 (2½) ins. k. 2, p. 2 rib, rows on right side having a k. 2 at each end.

Change to No. 8 needles and with right side facing, continue in rib, shaping shoulder edge and underarm by increasing 1 stitch at each end of next and every following 8th row until there are 52 sts. With wrong side facing, continue shaping underarm edge by increasing 1 stitch at beginning of next row, then at this edge on following 5 rows.

NEXT ROW: wrong side facing, cast on 15 (15), rib to end. NEXT ROW: Increase in 1st stitch, rib to end. Continue shaping for side edge by casting on 15 (15) sts. at beginning of next and following alternate row, then 10 (10) sts. at beginning of next 2 alternate rows. NEXT ROW: Increase in 1st stitch, rib to end: 125 (125) sts.

Work 11 (17) rows straight over all stitches, then with right side facing, shape shoulder edge by casting off 14 (14) sts. at beginning of next and following 4 alternate rows; cast off remaining 55 (55) sts. fairly loosely.

Front half of right sleeve and front panel: Work as for back half, reversing all shaping.

Back half of left sleeve and back panel: Work exactly as for front half of right sleeve and front panel.

Front half of left sleeve and front panel: Work exactly as for back half of right sleeve and back panel.

FRONT BORDERS AND NECKBAND

Borders: Left: With No. 10 needles, cast on 17 (17) sts. and work thus:—1ST ROW: right side facing, k. 8, sl. 1, k. 8. 2ND ROW: Purl. Repeat these 2 rows until strip fits up left front to start of neck shaping; leave stitches on a safety-pin.

Right: Work a similar piece for right front with the addition of 10 (10) buttonholes, first to come 1-inch from lower edge, 10th (10th) 2 rows below start of neck shaping and remainder evenly spaced between. First mark position of buttons on left front with pins to ensure even spacing, then work holes to correspond. To make a buttonhole:—right side facing, k. 3, cast off 3, k. 2, sl. 1, k. 2, cast off 3, k. 3. NEXT ROW: Purl, casting on 3 over those cast off.

12

Neckband: With right side facing and No. 10 needles, return to stitches of right front border, cast off 9, k. 8, rib 19 sts. from right front ribbing last 2 sts. together, rib 42 (42) from back of neck, ribbing first 2 sts. and last 2 sts. together, rib 19 from left front, ribbing first 2 sts. together, k. 8, sl. 1, k. 8 from left border.

NEXT ROW: Cast off 9, p. 8, k. 3, rib to last 11 sts., k. 3, p. 8. NEXT ROW: k. 8, p. 3, rib to last 11 sts., p. 3, k. 8: 92 (92) sts. Continue in rib, keeping 11 sts. at each end as before for a further 1⅜ ins.; cast off loosely.

TO MAKE UP

Press parts very lightly on wrong side, taking care not to spoil the ribbing and cables. Pin back half of sleeves and back panels in position to centre back piece from shoulder to lower edge, keeping 4 sts. free at lower edge of each side panel; turn these stitches under and slip-hem on wrong side. Pin front of sleeves and front side panels in position to fronts in the same way. Sew neatly in position on wrong side.

Join side and underarm seams; join shoulder seams of sleeves, taking care that they come in line with shoulder seams of main work. Fold front borders in half at slipped-stitch and sew in position to fronts. Fold neckband in half to wrong side and slip-hem; oversew round double buttonholes; sew on buttons and press stud at neck. Press all seams.

13

fair-isle bands on a white ground for a summer cardigan

MATERIALS: Of Patons Beehive Fingering 3-ply, Patonised, 7 ozs. white, 2 ozs. red, and 1 oz. each of blue and black. A pair each No. 10 and No. 11 "Beehive" needles. Seven buttons.

MEASUREMENTS: To fit 34-inch bust; length from top of shoulders, 21 inches; sleeve seam, 17 inches.

TENSION: 8 stitches to an inch over Fair Isle.

N.B.—W. = white, R. = red, B. = blue, Bl. = black.

BACK

With No. 11 needles and white wool, cast on 123 sts. and work 5 rows stocking-stitch, starting with a knit row, to be turned up later for hem. NEXT ROW: Knit.

Change to No. 10 needles and pattern. 1ST ROW (right side facing): Knit in W. 2ND ROW: Purl * 1W., 1R., 2W., 1R., 1W.; repeat from * to last 3 sts., 1W., 1R., 1W. 3RD ROW: Knit * 1B., 1R., 1B., 3R.; repeat from * to last 3 sts., 1B., 1R., 1B.

4TH ROW: Purl * 1B., 1R., 2B., 1R., 1B.; repeat from * to last 3 sts., 1B., 1R., 1B. 5TH ROW: Knit * 1Bl., 1R., 1Bl.; repeat from * to end.

6TH, 7TH AND 8TH ROWS: As 4th, 3rd and 2nd in that order. 9TH, 10TH AND 11TH ROWS: Knit in W. 12TH ROW: Purl in W. 13TH AND 14TH ROWS: As 11th and 12th.

15TH ROW: Knit * 3W., 2R.; repeat from * to last 3 sts., 3W. 16TH ROW: Purl * 3W., 2R.; repeat from * to last 3 sts., 3W. 17TH–20TH ROWS: Stocking-stitch

in W. 21ST AND 22ND ROWS: Knit in W. These 22 rows form pattern.

Continue in pattern, shaping side edges by decreasing 1 stitch at each end of next and every following 8th row, 5 times (113 sts.). Change to No. 11 needles and work straight to end of 3rd pattern.

Change back to No. 10 needles and continue in pattern, shaping side edges by increasing 1 stitch at each end of next and every following 4th row until there are 139 sts., taking increased stitches into pattern as they are made. Work straight until 16th row of 6th pattern has been done.

With right side facing, shape armholes by casting off 8 sts. at beginning of next 2 rows, then k. 2 tog. at each end of every row until 111 sts. remain. Work straight until 12th row of 9th pattern has been done.

With right side facing, shape shoulders by casting off 13 sts. at beginning of next 6 rows; cast off remainder.

FRONTS

Left: With No. 11 needles and white wool, cast on 63 sts. and work 5 rows stocking-stitch, starting with a knit row. NEXT ROW: Knit. Change to No. 10 needles and work 1 pattern as for back.

Continue in pattern, shaping side edge by k. 2 tog. at beginning of next and every following 8th row, 5 times (58 sts.). Change to No. 11 needles and work straight to end of 3rd pattern. Change back to No. 10 needles and shape side edge by increasing 1 stitch at beginning of next and every following 4th row until there are 71 sts. Work straight until front matches back.

With right side facing, shape armholes by casting off 8 sts. at beginning of next row, then k. 2 tog. at this edge on following 6 rows, then keep this edge straight. *At the same time,* shape front edge by k. 2 tog. at this edge on 1st and every following 3rd row until 39 sts. remain.

Work a few rows straight until front matches back, then shape shoulder by casting off 13 sts. at beginning of next 3 alternate rows, armhole edge.

Right: Work to correspond with left front, reversing shapings.

SLEEVES

With No. 11 needles and white wool, cast on 63 sts. and work 5 rows stocking-stitch, starting with a knit row. NEXT ROW: Knit. Now work 1 pattern as for back, then change to No. 10 needles and continue in pattern, increasing 1 stitch at each end of next and every following 6th row until there are 105 sts. Work straight until 16th row of 7th pattern has been done.

With right side facing, shape top by casting off 5 sts. at beginning of next 2 rows, then k. 2 tog. at each end of every alternate row until 61 sts. remain, then at each end of every row until 29 sts. remain. Cast off, taking 2 sts. tog. each time to last 3 sts., k. 3 tog.

RIBBED BAND

Join shoulder seams. With white wool and No. 11 needles, cast on 11 sts. and work a length in k. 1, p. 1 rib to fit up right front, round back of neck and down left front when slightly stretched. Make 7 buttonholes up right front; first comes in 3rd and 4th rows from bottom edge, last one at beginning of front slope, and remainder at equal intervals. First mark position of buttons with pins on left front, then work holes to correspond. To make a buttonhole:—Rib 4, cast off 3, rib to end and back, casting on 3 over those cast off.

TO MAKE UP

Press pieces well under a damp cloth. Join side and sleeve seams; sew in sleeves, matching patterns carefully. Turn under and hem stocking-stitch rows all round lower edge and cuffs. Sew on ribbed band; sew on buttons to match buttonholes.

15

a useful waistcoat-affair

MATERIALS: 8 ozs. Patons Beehive Fingering 3-ply, Patonised. A pair each No. 11 and No. 13 "Beehive" needles. Six buttons.

MEASUREMENTS: To fit 33–35-inch bust; length from top of shoulders to point, including ribbing, 20 inches; sleeve seams, 6 inches.

TENSION: 8 stitches and 10¼ rows to an inch over pattern.

BACK

With No. 11 needles, cast on 123 sts. and work in pattern thus:—1ST ROW: k. 4, * p. 1, knit into back and front of next stitch, p. 1, k. 4; repeat from * to end. 2ND ROW: p. 4, * k. 1, p. 2 tog., k. 1, p. 4; repeat from * to end. These 2 rows form pattern.

Repeat them for 2½ inches, then continue in pattern, increasing at each end of 3rd and every following 6th row until there are 137 sts. Work straight until back measures 9 inches.

With right side facing, shape armholes by casting off 9 sts. at beginning of next 2 rows, then k. 2 tog. at each end of every alternate row until 101 remain. Work straight until back measures 15½ inches, then shape shoulders by casting off 10 sts. at beginning of next 6 rows. Cast off remainder.

FRONTS

Begin by making pockets. With No. 11 needles, cast on 32 sts. and work 3 inches in pattern as for back, ending with a row on right side. Leave stitches on safety-pin and make 3 more pockets in the same way.

Right: With No. 11 needles, cast on 2 sts. 1ST ROW: Increase in 1st stitch, k.1. 2ND ROW: p.3. 3RD ROW: Increase in 1st stitch, k. 2. 4TH ROW: Cast on 3, k. 1, p. 1, k. 1, p. 3, increase in last stitch. 5TH ROW: Increase in 1st stitch, k. 4, p. 1, knit into back and front of next stitch, p. 1. 6TH ROW: Cast on 3, p. 3, k. 1, p. 2 tog., k. 1, p. 4, k. 1, increase in last stitch.

7TH ROW: Increase in 1st stitch, knit into back and front of next stitch, p. 1, k. 4, p. 1, knit into back and front of next stitch, p. 1, k. 3. 8TH ROW: Cast on 3, p. 1, k. 1, * p. 4, k. 1, p. 2 tog., k.1; repeat from * to last stitch, increase in last stitch.

9TH ROW: Increase in 1st stitch, k. 1, * p. 1, knit into back and front of next stitch, p. 1, k. 4; repeat from * to last 2 sts., p. 1, increase in last stitch. 10TH ROW: Cast on 3, p. 2, * k. 1, p. 2 tog., k. 1, p. 4; repeat from * to last 7 sts., k. 1, p. 2 tog., k. 1, p. 2, increase in last stitch. 11TH ROW: Increase in 1st stitch, k. 3, * p. 1, knit into back and front of next stitch, p. 1, k. 4; repeat from * to last 5 sts., p. 1, knit into back and front of next stitch, p. 1, k. 2. 12TH ROW: Cast on 2, * p. 4, k. 1, p. 2 tog., k. 1; repeat from * to last 5 sts., p. 4, k. 1 (26 sts.).

13TH ROW: Increase in 1st stitch, pattern to last stitch, increase in last stitch. 14TH ROW: Cast on 2, pattern to end. Repeat last 2 rows 8 times more (62 sts.). 31ST ROW: Pattern to last stitch, increase in last stitch (63 sts.).

Work 2½ inches straight in pattern. NEXT ROW (right side facing): Pattern 17, cast off 32

16

for pocket, pattern 14. NEXT ROW: Pattern back, working in pocket-stitches in place of those cast off.

Continue in pattern, increasing at side edge on next and every following 6th row until there are 70 sts., taking new stitches into pattern as they are made. Continue without shaping until straight edge at centre front measures 7¼ inches, ending at front edge. Start to slope front edge by k. 2 tog. at this edge on next and every following 3rd row until 66 sts. remain. With right side facing, work in top pocket thus:—Pattern 13, cast off 32, pattern to end and back, working in pocket-stitches over those cast off.

Now continue sloping front edge, but on every 4th row, and at the same time when side edge matches back, with wrong side facing, shape armhole by casting off 9 sts. at beginning of next row, then k. 2 tog. at this edge on following 9 alternate rows. Now keep armhole edge straight and continue sloping front edge on every 4th row as before until 30 sts. remain.

Work straight until front matches back, then shape shoulder by casting off 10 sts. at beginning of next 3 alternate rows, armhole edge.

Left: Work to correspond with right, reversing shapings. Remember to have front instead of back of work facing when casting on groups of 3 and 2 sts. for point shaping, so that fronts match. When introducing lower pocket, your first row will read: Right side facing, pattern 14, cast off 32, pattern 17.

SLEEVES

With No. 11 needles, cast on 91 sts. and work in pattern as for back, beginning and ending row with k. 2 instead of k. 4. Shape sides by increasing each end of 7th and every following 6th row until there are 105 sts. Work straight in pattern until sleeve measures 5 inches.

Shape top by k. 2 tog. at each end of every row until 25 sts. remain; cast off.

RIBBED BORDERS

Join side and shoulder seams. With No. 13 needles, begin at right front point. Cast on 2 sts. 1ST ROW (right side facing): Knit twice into 1st stitch p. 1. 2ND ROW: k. 1, p. 1, knit twice into last stitch. 3RD ROW: Knit twice into 1st stitch, p. 1, k. 1, p. 1. 4TH ROW: k. 1, p. 1, k. 1, p. 1, knit twice into last stitch. Continue increasing thus at one edge only on every row until there are 12 sts. Work straight in rib until piece fits all round lower edge, finishing at left front point. With right side facing, shape ribbing by k. 2 tog. at beginning of next row, then decrease 1 stitch at this edge on every row until 2 sts. remain; fasten off.

Sew border in position.

In the same way begin at left front point and work a strip to fit up left front, round back of neck and down right front. Sew in position as you go along and make 6 buttonholes down right front. Mark position of buttons on left front with pins, as shown in photograph, then work holes to correspond. To make a buttonhole:—Rib 4, cast off 4, rib to end and back, casting on 4 over those cast off. When buttonholes are done, work straight in rib to end of point, then shape ribbing as before.

With No. 13 needles, cast on 12 sts. and work a strip in k. 1, p. 1 rib to fit across each pocket top. In the same way make two more strips to go round bottom of each sleeve.

TO MAKE UP

Press pieces on wrong side under a damp cloth. Join sleeve seams; sew in sleeves. Stitch ribbed bands to pocket tops and round sleeves. Catch down pocket linings. Join sides of ribbing neatly at front points; sew on buttons.

Cardigan

Materials: Of Patons Double Quick
Knitting, 15/16/17/18 ozs. Rose Petal
207 and 3/3/3/3 ozs. White. A pair
each No. 8 and No. 10 "Queen Bee"
needles. 6 buttons.

Measurements: To fit 33–34/35–36/
37–38/39–40 inch bust; length from
top of shoulders, 23/23/23½/23½ ins.;
sleeve seam, 11/11/11½/11½ ins.

Tension: 5¼ sts. and 7½ rows to an
inch over stocking-stitch on No. 8
needles.

N.B.—R.=Rose Petal. W.=White.

BACK

With No. 10 needles and R. wool,
cast on 92/98/104/108 sts. and work
2½ ins. in stocking-stitch, ending with
a purl row. Make a hem on next row
by folding work in half, purl side
inside, and knitting 1 st. from needle
together with 1 st. from cast on edge
all along. NEXT ROW: purl, increasing
8/8/8/10 sts. evenly across: 100/106/
112/118 sts.

With right side facing, change to
No. 8 needles and continue straight
in stocking-stitch until back measures
14½/14/14/14 ins.

With right side facing, shape raglan
armholes by casting off 3/4/4/6 sts.
at beginning of next 2 rows.

NEXT ROW: k. 2, k. 2 tog., k. to last 4 sts., k. 2 tog.t.b.l., k. 2. NEXT ROW: purl. Repeat the last 2 rows until 6/6/6/6 sts. remain. NEXT ROW: purl. Cast off.

BORDER AND COLLAR

Border: With No. 10 needles and W. wool, cast on 19 sts. 1ST ROW: k. 9, slip 1 purlways, k. 9. 2ND ROW: purl. Repeat these 2 rows until border fits up right front, all round back of neck and down left front, when slightly stretched; making 6 double buttonholes up right front:—

First to come 1¼ ins. up from lower edge, and remaining 5 spaced at 2½ inch intervals. To make a double buttonhole:—right side facing, k. 3, cast off 3, k. 3, slip 1 purlways, k. 3, cast off 3, k. 3; purl back casting on 3 over those cast off. Sew one edge of border in position as you go along. Cast off.

Fold border in half to wrong side up to the slipped stitch and slip-hem neatly on wrong side so that stitches do not show through on right side of work. Oversew facing at lower edge. Oversew loosely round double buttonholes.

Collar: With No. 10 needles and R. wool, cast on 118/118/122/122 sts. and work 6 rows stocking-stitch, starting with a knit row, and increasing 1 st. at each end of every knit row: 124/124/128/128 sts. NEXT ROW: purl (this row forms ridge for hemline).

NEXT ROW: p. twice in 1st st., p. to last stitch, p. twice in last stitch. NEXT ROW: k. 1, slip 1, k. to last 2 sts., slip 1, k. 1. NEXT ROW: p. twice in 1st st., p. to last stitch, p. twice in last stitch. NEXT ROW: k. 2, slip 1, k. to last 3 sts., slip 1, k. 2. NEXT ROW: p. twice in 1st st., p. to last stitch, p. twice in last stitch: 130/130/134/134 sts.

NEXT ROW: k. 3, slip 1, k. to last 4 sts., slip 1, k. 3. NEXT ROW: purl. Repeat the last 2 rows until collar is 1½ ins. deep from purl ridge, ending with a purl row.

Continue as follows: NEXT ROW: k. 3 R., slip 1 purlways, k. 12 R., join in W., 98/98/102/102 W., join in 2nd ball R., k. 12 R., slip 1 purlways, k. 3 R. NEXT ROW: P., 16 R., 98/98/102/102 W., 16 R. Repeat the last 2 rows 4 times more, twisting wools on wrong side of work when changing colours to avoid a hole.

NEXT ROW: k. 3 R., slip 1 purlways, k. 12 R., k. 8 W., join in 3rd ball R. for centre stitches and k. 82/82/86/86, join in 2nd ball W. and k. 8, k. 12 R., slip 1, k. 3 R. NEXT ROW: P., 16 R., 8 W., 82/82/86/86 R, 8 W., 16 R. Repeat the last 2 rows, twisting wools on wrong side as before, until collar measures 4 ins. from purl ridge. Cast off.

TO MAKE UP

Press parts lightly on wrong side under a damp cloth. Join side and sleeve seams; insert sleeves.

Pocket Tops: With No. 10 needles and R. wool, rejoin wool to 24 pocket top stitches and work 4 rows k. 1, p. 1 rib. Cast off evenly in rib.

Catch down pocket linings neatly on wrong side and sew pocket tops in position to main work.

Join mitred corners of collar neatly. Turn under 6 rows of stocking-stitch to wrong side up to the purl ridge and 3 sts. up to the slipped stitch at sides of collar and slip-hem in position. Press hems. Sew collar neatly in position to neck edge taking care that ends are evenly matched on fronts. Press all seams. Sew on buttons.

NEXT ROW: k. 2, k. 2 tog., k. to last 4 sts., k. 2 tog. through back of loops, k. 2. NEXT ROW: purl. Repeat the last 2 rows until 28/28/30/32 sts. remain. NEXT ROW: purl. Cast off.

FRONTS

Start by making pocket linings. With No. 8 needles and R. wool, cast on 24 sts. and work 3½ ins. in stocking-stitch, ending with a purl row. Leave stitches on a spare needle. Make another piece the same.

Left: With No. 10 needles and R. wool, cast on 42/45/48/50 sts. and work 2½ ins. stocking-stitch, ending with a purl row. Make a hem on next row as for back. NEXT ROW: purl, increasing 4/4/4/5 sts. evenly across: 46/49/52/55 sts.

With right side facing, change to No. 8 needles and continue straight in stocking-stitch until front measures 4¾ ins., ending with a purl row.

Here introduce pocket. NEXT ROW: k. 10/11/12/13, slip next 24 sts. on a spare needle and in place of these, k. 24 sts. of one pocket lining, k. to end. NEXT ROW: purl. Work straight until front measures same as back at side edge.

With right side facing, shape raglan and neck edge. NEXT ROW: cast off 3/4/4/6, k. to last 2 sts., k. 2 tog. NEXT ROW: purl. NEXT ROW: k. 2, k. 2 tog., k. to end. Continue shaping raglan at beg. of every alternate row and *at the same time* shape neck edge by decreasing 1 st. at this edge on following 6th row, then on every following 8th row until 7/9/7/3 sts. remain.

Now keep neck edge straight but continue shaping raglan on alternate rows as before until 2 sts. remain. K. 2 tog. and fasten off.

Right: Work to correspond with left front, reversing shapings.

When introducing pocket this row will read:—right side facing, k. 12/14/16/18, slip next 24 sts. on a spare needle and in place of these, k. 24 sts. of pocket lining, k. to end.

SLEEVES

With No. 10 needles and R. wool, cast on 58/58/60/62 sts. and work 2 ins. k. 1, p. 1 rib.

With right side facing, change to No. 8 needles and stocking-stitch, starting with a knit row and shape sides by increasing 1 st. at each end of 7th and every following 8th row until there are 70/70/72/74 sts. Work straight until sleeve seam measures 11/11/11½/11½ ins.

With right side facing, shape top by casting off 3/4/4/5 sts. at beg. of next 2 rows. NEXT ROW: k. 2, k. 2 tog., k. to last 4 sts., k. 2 tog. through back of loops, k. 2. Work 3 rows straight. Repeat the last 4 rows 3/6/7/7 times more.

19

WHITE CARDIGAN-JUMPER

Materials: 10 (11) ozs. White and 1 (1) oz. Viridian 160 in Patons Beehive Fingering 3-ply, Patonised. A pair each No. 10 and No. 12 "Queen Bee" needles. A No. 13 crochet hook. 16-inch zip-fastener. Small hook and eye.

Measurements : To fit 33-34 (35-36)-inch bust; length from top of shoulders, 22½ (22½) inches; sleeve seam, 13 (13) inches.

Tension: Equivalent to 7½ sts. and 9½ rows to an inch over stocking-stitch.

N.B. — Instructions for large size given in brackets thus ( ). Where one set of figures is given, this applies to both sizes. Figures in brackets thus [ ] also apply to both sizes.

Abbreviations: W. = White, V. = Viridian.

BACK

With No. 10 needles and white wool, cast on 129 (137) sts. and work in mock cable pattern as follows:—1ST ROW: right side facing, k. 4, * p. 1, k. 3; repeat from * to last stitch, k. 1. 2ND ROW: * k. 1, p. 3; repeat from * to last stitch, k. 1. 3RD ROW: k. 1, wool forward, k. 3, pass the wool forward over the k. 3. * p. 1, wool over needle, k. 3, pass the wool over needle over the k. 3; repeat from * to last stitch, k. 1. 4TH ROW: * k. 1, p. 3; repeat from * to last stitch, k. 1. These 4 rows form pattern.

Work a further 4 rows in pattern, then continue in pattern, decreasing 1 stitch at each end of next and every following 8th row until 121 (129) sts. remain. Work 26 rows straight in pattern.

With wrong side facing, decrease for waist as follows:— [k. 1, p. 3] twice (4 times), * k. 1, p. 1, p. 2 tog., [k. 1, p. 3] twice; repeat from * to last 5 sts., k. 1, p. 1, p. 2 tog., k. 1, [111 (119) sts.]. Change to No. 12 needles.

NEXT ROW: * k. 1, p. 1; repeat from * to last stitch, k. 1. NEXT ROW: p. 1, * k. 1, p. 1; repeat from * to end. Repeat these 2 rows until waist ribbing measures 2 inches, increasing 10 (10) sts. evenly across on last row [121 (129) sts.].

With right side facing, change back to No. 10 needles and pattern, starting with 1st pattern row, and shaping sides by increasing 1 stitch at each end of 3rd and every following 4th row until there are 145 (153) sts., taking increased sts. into pattern as they are made. Work straight until back measures 15 inches ending with 4th pattern row.

With right side facing, shape armholes by casting off 8 sts. at beginning of next 2 rows, then decrease 1 stitch at each end of next and every alternate row until 113 (121) sts. remain. Continue straight in pattern until armhole measures 7¼ inches.

With right side facing, shape shoulders as follows:—1ST AND 2ND ROWS: Pattern to last 13 (16) sts., turn. 3RD AND 4TH ROWS: Pattern to last 25 (28) sts., turn. 5TH AND 6TH ROWS: Pattern to last 41 (44) sts., turn. 7TH ROW: Pattern to end. Cast off.

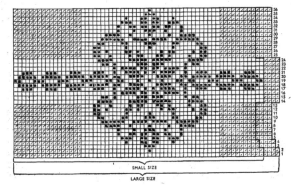

SMALL SIZE

LARGE SIZE

22

FRONTS

Pocket Linings: With No. 10 needles and white wool, cast on 41 (41) sts. and repeat the 4 rows of mock cable pattern 10 times, then 1st and 2nd rows again. Break wool and leave sts. on a spare needle. Work another piece the same.

Left: With No. 10 needles and white wool, cast on 77 (81) sts. and work 8 rows in mock cable pattern, then continue in pattern, shaping side edge by decreasing 1 stitch at beginning of next and every following 8th row until 73 (77) sts. remain. Work 3 rows straight in pattern.

Here introduce pocket top. 1ST ROW: Pattern 18 (22), k. 37; pattern 18 (18). 2ND ROW: Pattern 18 (18), p. 37, pattern 18 (22). 3RD ROW: Pattern 18 (22), knit, 2 W., join in viridian, [3 V., 3 W] 5 times, 3 V., 2 W., pattern 18 (18). 4TH ROW: Pattern 18 (18), purl, [1 W., 5 V.] 6 times, 1 W., pattern 18 (22). 5TH ROW: Pattern 18 (22), knit, 2 V., [3 W., 3 V] 5 times, 3 W., 2 V., pattern 18 (18). 6TH ROW: As 4th. 7TH ROW: As 3rd. Break V. wool. 8TH ROW: As 2nd. 9TH ROW: As 1st. 10TH ROW: Pattern 16 (16), cast off 41, pattern 16 (20). 11TH ROW: In pattern, working across the pocket lining sts. in place of those cast off.

Work 12 rows straight in pattern. With wrong side facing, decrease for waist as follows:—[k. 1, p. 3] twice (3 times), [k. 1, p. 1, p. 2 tog.] 6 (6) times, [k. 1, p. 3] twice (twice), [k. 1, p. 1, p. 2 tog.] 6 (6) times, [k. 1, p. 3] twice (twice), k. 1 [61 (65) sts.].

Change to No. 12 needles. NEXT ROW: * k. 1, p. 1; repeat from * to last stitch, k. 1. NEXT ROW: * p. 1, k. 1; repeat from * to last stitch, p. 1. Repeat these 2 rows until waist ribbing measures 2 inches, increasing 4 (4) sts. evenly across on last row [65 (69) sts.].

With right side facing, change back to No. 10 needles and pattern, shaping side edge by increasing 1 stitch at beginning of 3rd and every following 4th row until there are 77 (81) sts. into pattern as they are made. Work straight until front measures 15 inches, ending with 4th pattern row.

With right side facing, shape armholes by casting off 12 (12) sts. at beginning of next row, then decrease 1 stitch at this edge on every alternate row until 60 (64) sts. remain. Pattern back.

Here introduce motif across yoke. The shaded parts on chart (see page 19) represent the mock cable pattern, blank squares are stocking-stitch in white and solid squares are stocking-stitch in viridian. Work the first 6 rows as follows:— 1ST ROW: k. 2 tog., k. 1, [p. 1, k. 3] twice (3 times), p. 1, k. 6, [increase in next stitch, k. 5] 3 (3) times, increase in next stitch, k. 6, [p. 1, k. 3] 4 (4) times, k. 1 [63 (67) sts.]. 2ND ROW: Pattern 17, purl, 17 W., 1 V., 17 W., pattern 11 (15).

3RD ROW: k. 2 tog., p. 1, pattern 8 (12), knit, 16 W., 3 V., 16 W., pattern 17. 4TH ROW: Pattern 17, purl, 11 W., 1 V., 3 W., 2 V., 1 W., 2 V., 3 W., 1 V., 11 W., pattern 10 (14). 5TH ROW: k. 2 tog., k. 1, pattern 7 (11), knit, 10 W., 3 V., 2 W., 2 V., 1 W., 2 V., 3 V., 10 W., pattern 17. 6TH ROW: Pattern 17, purl, 9 W., 1 V., 2 W., 2 V., [1 W., 2 V.] 3 (3) times, 2 W., 1 V., 9 W., pattern 9 (13).

Continue in pattern from chart, working rows 7–13 inclusive. 14TH ROW: Purl, 21 W., 4 V., 4 W., 5 V., 1 W., 5 V., 4 W., 4 V., 6 W., purl twice in next stitch in W., 3 W., purl twice in next stitch in W., 2 (6) W. [63 (67) sts.]. Now work rows 15–23 inclusive from chart. 24TH ROW: Purl, 21 W., 4 V., 4 W., 5 V., 1 W., 5 V., 4 W, 4 V., 6 W., p. 2 tog. W., 3 W., p. 2 tog. W., 2 (6) W. Now work rows 25–36 inclusive from chart. 37TH ROW: Pattern 9 (13), k. 6, [k. 2 tog., k. 5] 3 (3) times, k. 2 tog., k. 6, pattern 17 [57 (61) sts.]. 38TH ROW: k. 1, [p. 3, k. 1] 14 (15) times. 39TH ROW: k. 1, wl. fwd., k. 3, pass the wl. fwd. over the k. 3, [p. 1, w.o.n., k. 3, pass the w.o.n. over the k. 3] 13 (14) times, k. 1.

Continue in mock cable pattern and work 8 rows straight. With wrong side facing, shape neck by casting off 8 (9) sts. at beginning of next row, then k. 2 tog. at neck edge on every row until 41 (44) sts. remain. Work a few rows straight until front matches back.

With wrong side facing, shape shoulder as follows:—Pattern to last 13 (16) sts., turn and pattern back; pattern to last 25 (28) sts., turn and pattern back. Cast off.

23

Materials: Of Patons Beehive Fingering 3-ply, Patonised, 8 (9) ozs. Sunglint 101, and a small ball (less than ½-oz.) of the same wool in White. A pair each No. 13 and No. 11 "Queen Bee" needles. A No. 12 crochet hook. Ten small buttons.

Measurements: To fit 34–35 (36–37) inch bust; length from top of shoulders, 20 (20½) ins.; sleeve seam, 14½ (14½) ins. cuff turned down.

Tension: 8 sts. and 10 rows to an inch over stocking-stitch on No. 11 needles.

Abbreviations: Tw.2B. = knit into back of 2nd stitch on left hand needle, then knit into front of 1st stitch and slip both stitches off together; Tw.2F. = knit into front of 2nd stitch on left hand needle, then knit into front of 1st stitch and slip both stitches off together; Y. = Sunglint; W. = White.

Gay as a buttercup
in bright yellow
and white

N.B.—*Instructions for large size given in brackets thus ( ). Where one set of figures is given this applies to both sizes.*

CARDIGAN WITH CROCHET BORDERS

BACK

With No. 13 needles and Y. wool, cast on 122 (130) sts. and work 1 inch k. 1, p. 1 rib, increasing 9 sts. evenly across on last row as follows:—rib 9, * increase in next stitch, rib 12 (13); repeat from * to last 9 sts., increase in next stitch, rib 8: 131 (139) sts.

Change to No. 11 needles and pattern as follows:—1st row: right side facing, k. 2, Tw.2B., Tw.2F., p. 5, k. 5 (7), p. 5, * Tw.2B., Tw.2F., p. 5, k. 17 (19), p. 5, Tw.2B., Tw.2F., p. 5, * k. 9, p. 5, repeat from * to * once, k. 5 (7), p. 5, Tw.2B., Tw.2F., k. 2. 2nd row: k. 2, p. 4, k. 5, p. 5 (7), k. 5, * p. 4, k. 5, p. 17 (19), k. 5, p. 4, k. 5, * p. 9, k. 5, repeat from * to * once, p. 5 (7), k. 5, p. 4, k. 2. 3rd row: k. 2, Tw.2F., Tw.2B., p. 5, k. 5 (7), p. 5, * Tw.2F., Tw.2B., p. 5, k. 17 (19), p. 5, Tw.2F., Tw.2B., p. 5, * k. 9, p. 5, repeat from * to * once, k. 5 (7), p. 5, Tw.2F., Tw.2B., k. 2. 4th row: as 2nd. These 4 rows form pattern.

Work straight in pattern until back measures 4 ins. at centre. With right side facing, start to shape sides on next row as follows:—pattern 11, increase in next stitch, pattern to last 12 sts., increase in next stitch, pattern to end. next row: k. 2, p. 4, k. 5, p. 6 (8), k. 5, * p. 4, k. 5, p. 17 (19), k. 5, p. 4, k. 5, * p. 9, k. 5, repeat from * to * once, p. 6 (8), k. 5, p. 4, k. 2. Continue thus shaping sides by increasing 1 stitch inside the first and last 11 sts. on 4th and every following 6th row until there are 155 (163) sts., taking increased stitches into stocking-stitch panel as they are made. Work straight until back measures 12½ (12½) ins. at centre.

With right side facing, shape armholes by casting off 5 sts. at beginning of next 2 rows. next row: k. 2, p. 4, k. 1, pattern to last 7 sts., k. 1, p. 4, k. 2. Repeat last 2 rows until 111 (115) sts. remain. Stitches in shaped stocking-stitch panels have now been decreased. Work straight until back measures 20 (20½) ins.

With right side facing, shape shoulders by casting off 11 (12) sts. at beginning of next 4 rows, then 11 (11) sts. at beginning of following 2 rows. Cast off remaining stitches.

FRONTS

Left: With No. 13 needles and Y. wool cast on 62 (66) sts. and work 1 inch k. 1, p. 1 rib. Change to No. 11 needles and pattern as follows:—1st row: right side facing, k. 2, Tw.2B., Tw.2F., p. 5, k. 5 (7), p. 5, Tw.2B., Tw.2F., p. 5, k. 17 (19), p. 5, Tw.2B., Tw.2F., p. 5, k. 1. 2nd row: k. 6, p. 4, k. 5, p. 17 (19), k. 5, p. 4, k. 5, p. 5 (7), k. 5, p. 4, k. 2. 3rd row: k. 2, Tw.2F., Tw.2B., p. 5, k. 5 (7), p. 5, Tw.2F., Tw.2B., p. 5, k. 17 (19), p. 5, Tw.2F., Tw.2B., p. 5, k. 1. 4th row: As 2nd.

Work straight in pattern until front measures 4 ins. at centre. With right side facing, shape side edge by increasing 1 stitch inside the first 11 sts. as for back, on next and every following 6th row until there are 74 (78) sts. Work straight until front matches back, then with right side facing, shape armhole by casting off 5 sts. at beginning of next row. next row: In pattern. next row: k. 2, Twist patt. 4, p. 2 tog., pattern to end. next row: Pattern to last 7 sts., k. 1, p. 4, k. 2. Continue in pattern, keeping a twist panel at armhole edge as for back, and shaping armhole by deceasing 1 stitch inside the first 6 sts. as before on next and every following alternate row until 52 (54) sts. remain. Work straight until front measures 17½ (18) ins. at centre.

With wrong side facing, shape neck by casting off 6 sts. at beginning of next row, then decrease 1 stitch at this edge on every row until 33 (35) sts. remain. Work straight until front matches back.

With right side facing, shape shoulder by casting off 11 (12) sts. at beginning of next and following alternate row, then 11 (11) sts. at beginning of following alternate row, armhole edge.

Right: Work to correspond with left front reversing shapings.

SLEEVES

With No. 13 needles and Y. wool cast on 76 (82) sts. and work 2½ ins. k. 1, p. 1 rib, increasing 1 stitch at end of last row: 77 (83) sts. Change to No. 11 needles and pattern. Your first 2 rows will read:—1st row: right side facing, k. 2, Tw.2B., Tw.2F., p. 5, k. 5 (7), p. 5, Tw.2B., Tw.2F., p. 5, k. 17 (19), p. 5, Tw.2B., Tw.2F., p. 5, k. 5 (7), p. 5, Tw.2B., Tw.2F., k. 2. 2nd row: k. 2, p. 4, k. 5, p. 5 (7), k. 5, p. 4, k. 5, p. 17 (19), k. 5, p. 4, k. 5, p. 5 (7), k. 5, p. 4, k. 2.

Continue in pattern shaping sleeve by increasing 1 stitch inside the first and last 11 sts. as for back on 7th and every following 8th row until there are 101 (107) sts. Work straight until sleeve seam measures 14½ (14½) ins.

With right side facing, shape top by casting off 5 sts. at beginning of next 2 rows. next row: k. 2, twist patt. 4, p. 2 tog., pattern to last 8 sts., p. 2 tog., twist patt. 4, k. 2. next row: k. 2, p. 4, k. 1, pattern to last 7 sts., k. 1, p. 4, k. 2. Continue thus decreasing 1 stitch at each side as for back on next and every following alternate row until 39 (41) sts. remain, keeping a twist panel at armhole edge throughout. Cast off 2 (2) sts. at beginning of next 6 rows; cast off remaining stitches.

FRONT BORDERS AND NECKBAND

Borders: Join shoulder seams. *Left:* With right side facing and Y. wool, work a row of double crochet down front edge; turn and work back increasing 1 stitch at end of row, neck edge. Join in W., and work in stripes of 2 rows W., 2 rows Y., 2 rows W., 2 rows Y., 2 rows W., increasing 1 stitch at neck edge on every row. Fasten off. *Right:* Work to correspond with left border, but with the addition of 10 buttonholes which are worked in 7th row. First buttonhole to come ¼-inch from lower edge, 10th to come 1-inch below start of neck shaping and remainder spaced evenly between. First mark position of buttons on left front with pins then work holes to correspond. To make a buttonhole, make 3 chain, miss 3 double crochet.

26

Neckband: In the same way, work 12 rows double crochet in stripes as before, all round neck, increasing 1 stitch at each end of every row.

TO MAKE UP

Press parts lightly on wrong side under a damp cloth. Join side and sleeve seams; insert sleeves. Join mitred corners of front border to neckband neatly. Sew on buttons to match buttonholes.

MATERIALS: 9 ozs. Patons Beehive Fingering, 3-ply ("Patonised" shrink-resist finish). A pair each No. 10 and No. 12 "Beehive" needles. A cable needle. Seven buttons.

MEASUREMENTS: To fit 34–36-inch bust; length from top of shoulders, 20 inches; sleeve seam, 5 inches.

TENSION: 7½ stitches to an inch across plain part of pattern on No. 10 needles.

BACK

With No. 10 needles, cast on 113 sts. and work 1 row k. 1, p. 1 rib. Start pattern. 1ST ROW (right side facing): p. 4, * k. 4, p. 6, make a bobble in next st. thus:— (p. 1, k. 1) four times into next st., thus making 8 loops on right needle; now slip 7th loop over 8th, 6th over 8th, 5th over 8th, and so on until only the 8th loop remains; purl this loop to close bobble; p. 6, k. 4; repeat from * four times more, p. 4.

2ND ROW: k. 4, * p. 4, k. 13, p. 4; repeat from * four times more, k. 4. 3RD ROW: p. 4, * slip next 4 on cable needle and place to front, p.1, k. 4 from cable needle, p. 11, slip next st. on cable needle and place to back, k. 4, then purl slipped st.; repeat from * four times more, p. 4. 4TH ROW: k. 4, * k. 1, p. 4, k. 11, p. 4, k. 1; repeat from * four times more, k. 4. 5TH ROW: p. 4, * p. 1, slip next 4 to front, p. 1, knit slipped sts., p. 9, slip next st. to back, k. 4, purl slipped st., p. 1, repeat from * four times more, p. 4. 6TH ROW: k. 4, * k. 2, p. 4, k. 9, p. 4, k. 2; repeat from * four times more, k. 4. 7TH ROW: p. 4, * p. 2, slip 4 to front, p. 1, knit slipped sts., p. 7, slip 1 to back, k. 4, purl slipped st., p. 2; repeat from * four times more, p. 4. 8TH ROW: k. 4, * k. 3, p. 4, k. 7, p. 4, k. 3; repeat from * four times more, k. 4. 9TH ROW: p. 4, * p. 3, slip 4 to front, p. 1, knit slipped sts., p. 2, make a bobble, p. 2, slip 1 to back, k. 4, purl slipped st., p. 3; repeat from * four times more, p. 4.
10TH ROW: k. 4, * k. 4, p. 4, k. 5, p. 4, k. 4; repeat

from * four times more, k. 4. 11TH ROW: p. 4, * p. 4, slip 4 to front, p. 1, knit slipped sts., p. 3, slip 1 to back, k. 4, purl slipped st., p. 4; repeat from * four times more, p. 4. 12TH ROW: k. 4, * k. 5, p. 4, k. 3, p. 4, k. 5; repeat from * four times more, k. 4. 13TH ROW: p. 4, * p. 5, slip 4 to front, p. 1, knit slipped sts., p. 1, slip 1 to back, k. 4, purl slipped st., p. 5; repeat from * four times more, p.4. 14TH ROW: k. 4, * k. 6, p. 4, k. 1, p. 4, k. 6; repeat from * four times more, k.4. 15TH ROW: p. 4, * p. 6, slip 5 to back, k. 4, knit 5 slipped sts., p. 6; repeat from * four times more, p. 4. 16TH ROW: k. 4, * k. 6, p. 4, k. 1, p. 4, k. 6; repeat from * four times more, k. 4. 17TH ROW: p. 4, * p. 5, slip 1 to back, k. 4, purl slipped st., p. 1, slip 4 to front, p. 1, knit 4 slipped sts., p. 5; repeat from * four times more, p. 4. 18TH ROW: k. 4, * k. 5, p. 4, k. 3, p. 4, k. 5; repeat from * four times more, k. 4. 19TH ROW: p. 4, * p. 4, slip 1 to back, k. 4, purl slipped st., p. 1, make a bobble, p. 1, slip 4 to front, p. 1, knit slipped sts., p. 4; repeat from * four times more, p. 4. 20TH ROW: k. 4, * k. 4, p. 4, k. 5, p. 4, k. 4; repeat from * four times more, k. 4. 21ST ROW: p. 4, * p. 3, slip 1 to back, k. 4, purl slipped st., p. 5, slip 4 to front, p. 1, knit 4 slipped sts., p. 3; repeat from * four times more, p. 4.

22ND ROW: k. 4, * k. 3, p. 4, k. 7, p. 4, k. 3; repeat from * four times more, k. 4. 23RD ROW: p. 4, * p. 2, slip 1 to back, k. 4, purl slipped st., p. 7, slip 4 to front, p. 1, knit slipped sts., p. 2; repeat from * four times more, p. 4.

24TH ROW: k. 4, * k. 2, p. 4, k. 9, p. 4, k. 2; repeat from * four times more, p. 4. 25TH ROW: p. 4, * p. 1, slip 1 to back, k. 4, purl slipped st., p. 9, slip 4 to front, p. 1, knit slipped sts., p. 2, slip 1 to back, k. 4, purl slipped st., p. 9, slip 4 to front, p. 1, knit slipped sts., p. 1; repeat from * twice more, p. 4.

26TH ROW: k. 4, * k. 1, p. 4, k. 11, p. 4, k. 1; repeat from * four times more, k. 4.

27TH ROW: p. 4, * slip 1 to back, k. 4, purl slipped st., p. 5, make a bobble, p. 5, slip 4 to front, p. 1, knit slipped sts.; repeat from * four times more, p. 4.

Repeat this pattern throughout, from 2nd to 27th rows inclusive. Continue in pattern until side edge measures 3 inches, then, keeping continuity of pattern, increase at each end of next and every following 4th row until there are 155 sts. on needle (when you have finished increases you will have one extra complete diamond pattern at each end). Work straight until side edge measures 12 inches.

Shape armholes by casting off 8 at beginning of next 2 rows, then k. 2 tog. at each end of every alternate row until 127 sts. remain. Work straight in pattern until back measures 19¾ inches, then shape shoulders by casting off 13 at beginning of next 6 rows; cast off remaining sts.

FRONTS

Left: With No. 10 needles, cast on 69 sts. and work 1 row k. 1, p. 1 rib, then continue in pattern as given for back but with 2 purl sts. at one end of the needle instead of 4, for centre front edge, thus:—1ST ROW: p. 4, work from * on 1st row of pattern three times, p. 2. 2ND ROW: k. 2, work from * on 2nd row three times, k. 4.

Continue in pattern for 3 inches, then increase at side edge only on next and every following 4th row until there are 90 sts. (One extra diamond pattern increased up side edge.) Work straight until side edge measures 12 inches, then cast off 8 on next row, side edge, and continue to decrease every other row at this side until 76 remain.

Work straight until front edge measures 17¼ inches, ending at straight edge. With back of work facing, cast off 8 at neck edge, then continue in p   decreasing 2 sts. at neck edge on every row until 39 sts. remain. (One decrease only on last row.)

Continue straight in pattern until front is same length as back, then shape shoulder by casting off 13 at beginning of next 3 alternate rows, armhole side.

Right: Work to correspond with left, reversing shapings.

BORDERS: With No. 12 needles, cast on 9 sts. and work a length of moss-stitch to reach up left side of front, when very slightly stretched. Do not cast off, but press and stitch to left front, leaving sts. on a small needle.

Join shoulder seams, then continue with moss border, shaping for corner thus:—Starting at outer edge of work, moss 7, turn and moss back; moss 5, turn and moss back; moss 3, turn and moss back.

Continue in moss-stitch until this last straight piece stretches all round neck; sew it to neck edge, then turn other corner thus:—Start at side edge of band, work as for first corner. Now work another long strip of moss-stitch as for left front and cast off. Stitch this piece to right front, but leave 7 spaces unstitched for buttonholes at even intervals. Work round these spaces in buttonhole to strengthen.

SLEEVES

With No. 10 needles, cast on 92 sts.   Work 1 row k. 1,
p. 1 rib, then change to pattern as for back, thus:—p. 4, repeat
from * four times, p. 4. Continue in pattern, increasing at each end
of every 4th row until there are 112 sts., keeping increased sts.
in reverse stocking-stitch.

Sleeve should now measure 4 inches, if not, work a few
rows straight, then shape top by casting off 4 at beginning
of next 2 rows, then 1 at each end of every alternate row
until 100 remain.

Decrease at each end of every 4th row until 88 remain, then
work straight until 4th cable twist is done.   Decrease at each
end of every alternate row until 78 remain.   Cast off 3 at beginning of next 6 rows.   NEXT ROW: k. 4, k. 2 tog. alternately
all along.   Cast off.

With No. 12 needles, cast on 9 sts. and work a band of
moss-stitch to go all round bottom of each sleeve. Cast off.

TO MAKE UP

Press pieces lightly on wrong side under a damp cloth.   Join
side and sleeve seams, after sewing band round bottom of sleeve.
Insert sleeves, gathering any fullness to top of shoulders.
Sew on buttons.

31

Warm Cable & moss stitch ribs

MATERIALS: Of Patons Beehive Fingering, 3-ply ("Patonised" shrink-resist finish), 8 ozs. for short sleeves, 10 ozs. long sleeves. A pair each No. 9 and No. 12 "Beehive" needles. Cable needle. Nine buttons.

MEASUREMENTS: To fit 33–35-inch bust; length from top of shoulders, 21½ inches; sleeve seam, 6 or 18½ inches.

TENSION: 7 stitches to an inch over moss panels, unpressed.

BACK

With No. 12 needles, cast on 121 sts. and work 14 rows k. 1, p. 1 rib. Change to No. 9 needles and pattern. 1ST ROW: k. 1, p. 1, k. 1, * p. 2, k. 6, p. 2 (k. 1, p. 1), twice, k. 1; repeat from * ending last repeat, p. 2, k. 6, p. 2, k. 1, p. 1, k. 1. 2ND ROW: k. 1, p. 1, k. 1, * k. 2, p. 6, k. 2, moss 5; repeat from * ending row moss 3 instead of moss 5. Repeat these 2 rows again.

5TH ROW: Moss 3, * p. 2, slip next 3 sts. on spare needle and place to back of work, k. 3, then k. 3 from spare needle, p. 2, moss 5; repeat from * ending row moss 3 instead of moss 5. 6TH ROW: As 2nd. These 6 rows form pattern. Repeat them five

times more. Change to No. 12 needles and work 2 inches in k. 1, p. 1 rib. Change to No. 9 needles and continue in pattern until side edge measures 14 inches.

With right side facing, shape armholes by casting off 5 sts. at beginning of next 2 rows, then decrease at each end of every alternate row until 99 sts. remain. Work straight until back measures 21 inches, then shape shoulders by casting off 10 sts. at beginning of next 6 rows. Cast off.

FRONTS

Left: With No. 12 needles, cast on 58 sts. and work 14 rows k. 1, p. 1 rib. Change to No. 9 needles and pattern. 1ST ROW (Right side facing) will read thus:—k. 1, p. 1, k. 1, * p. 2, k. 6, p. 2 (k. 1, p. 1), twice, k. 1, repeat from * ending last repeat, p. 2, k. 6, p. 2. 2ND ROW: k. 2, p. 6, k. 2 * moss 5, k. 2, p. 6, k. 2; repeat from * ending moss 3 instead of moss 5. Continue in pattern with waist rib until armhole is reached.

NEXT ROW (Right side facing): Cast off 5, then decrease at this edge on next 6 alternate rows. (47 sts.) Work straight until front measures 19 inches, ending at neck edge.

Now cast off 5 sts. at the beginning of the next two alternate rows, then k. 2 tog. at this edge on every row until 30 sts. remain. Work straight until front is same length as back, then shape shoulder by casting off 10 sts. at beginning of the next 3 alternate rows, armhole edge.

Right: Work to correspond with left, reversing shapings, and starting pattern so that front edges match as follows:—1ST ROW: (Right side facing.) p. 2, k. 6, p. 2, * moss 5, p. 2, k. 6, p. 2; repeat from * ending moss 3 instead of moss 5. 2ND ROW: Moss 3, * k. 2, p. 6, k. 2 moss 5; repeat from * ending k. 2, p. 6, k. 2.

BORDERS

With No. 12 needles, cast on 12 sts. and work a length of k. 1, p. 1 rib to go up left front when slightly stretched. Sew to front edge. Work a similar piece to go up right front, but with 9 buttonholes. Before starting, mark position of buttons on left front with pins, then work holes to correspond.

To make a buttonhole:—Rib 4, cast off 4, rib 4. On next row cast on 4 to replace those cast off.

COLLAR

With No. 12 needles, cast on 140 sts. and work 2¾ inches k. 1, p. 1 rib; cast off in rib.

SLEEVES

Short: With No. 12 needles, cast on 91 sts. and work 1 inch k. 1, p. 1 rib. Change to No. 9 needles and pattern as for back and work straight until sleeve measures 6 inches. Shape top by decreasing at each end of every alternate row until 61 remain, then at each end of every row until 21 remain. Cast off.

Long: With No. 12 needles, cast on 61 sts. and work 3 inches k. 1, p. 1 rib. Change to No. 9 needles and pattern as for back, increasing at each end of 7th and every following 6th row until there are 91 sts. Work straight until side edge measures 18¼ inches, then shape top as for short sleeves.

TO MAKE UP

Do not press. Join side, shoulder and sleeve seams; insert sleeves. Stitch collar carefully to neck edge, about ½ inch in from ribbed borders. Sew on buttons.

TENSION: 7½ stitches and 10 rows to an inch over stocking-stitch.

N.B.—When changing colour, twist wools round each other at back of work to avoid a hole.

MATERIALS: **7 ozs.** main shade and **3 ozs.** contrast of Patons Beehive Fingering 3-ply, Patonised. A pair each No. 10 and No. 12 "Beehive" needles. Eight buttons.

MEASUREMENTS: To fit 34–36-inch bust; length from top of shoulders, 23 inches; sleeve seam, 11 inches

FRONTS

Right: With No. 10 needles and dark shade, cast on 50 sts. Turn chart A sideways and work the 16 rows in stocking-stitch, odd rows knit, reading from right to left, and even rows purl, from left to right, and *at the same time* cast on 2 sts. at beginning of every knit row, front edge, in dark shade, thereafter take them into main shade, so that you have an edging in dark shade up front shaping. When the 16 rows are done you will have 66 sts. on needle.

Now work the 50 rows from chart A in vertical position, thus:—Work the required number of stitches in dark shade, then leave wool hanging and work to end in main shade, picking up dark shade again on the return row. *At the same time* shape side edge by decreasing 1 stitch at end of 1st and every following 4th row until 58 sts. remain. Work 7 rows straight.

Continue working pattern up front edge and shaping side edge by increasing at end of next and every following 6th row until there are 66 sts. Work straight until 17th row of 3rd pattern has been done.

With wrong side facing, shape armhole by casting off 6 sts. at beginning of next row, then k. 2 tog. at this edge on every row until 52 sts. remain. Work straight to end of 32nd

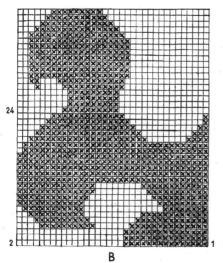

B

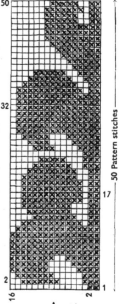

A

35

row of 3rd pattern, then continue working from chart B. When 24th row of chart B has been done, with right side facing, shape neck by casting off 7 sts. at beginning of next row, then k. 2 tog. at this edge on every alternate row. When chart B is done, continue in main shade, still decreasing at neck edge until 33 sts. remain. Work a few rows straight until armhole measures 7½ inches. With wrong side facing, shape shoulder by casting off 11 sts. at beginning of next and following 2 alternate rows, armhole edge.

Left: Work to correspond with right front, reversing shapings and charts, *i.e.*, knit rows will read from left to right and purl rows from right to left.

BACK

With dark shade and No. 10 needles, cast on 120 sts. Turn chart A sideways and work the 16 rows thus:—ODD ROWS: Knit, over first 60 sts. to bring you to centre back, k. 50 sts. from chart, then first 10 sts. again. To reverse pattern for second half, work first 10 sts. again, then the 50 sts., reading chart backwards. EVEN ROWS: Purl, reading sts. and chart in exactly the same way as given for odd rows.

Now continue in main shade, decreasing 1 stitch at each end of next and every following 4th row, 8 times in all (104 sts.). Work 7 rows straight, then increase at each end of next and every following 6th row until there are 120 sts.

Work straight until side edge matches front, then with right side facing, shape armholes by casting off 6 sts. at beginning of next 2 rows, then k. 2 tog. at each end of every row until 92 sts. remain.

Work straight until back matches fronts, then shape shoulders by casting off 11 sts. at beg. of next 6 rows. Cast off.

SLEEVES

With dark shade and No. 10 needles, cast on 100 sts. Turn chart A sideways. Work the 50 sts. once, then repeat them, reading row backwards.

When the 16 pattern rows are done, continue in main shade, but on first row decrease 4 sts. evenly across. Work straight on these 96 sts. until sleeve measures 11 inches.

Shape top by casting off 6 sts. at beginning of next 2 rows, then k. 2 tog. at beginning of every row until 28 sts. remain. Cast off.

RIBBED BANDS

Press pieces well under a- damp cloth. *Neck:* Join shoulder seams. With dark shade and No. 12 needles, cast on 13 sts. and work a strip in k. 1, p. 1 rib to fit round neck. Sew in position as you go along for a good fit. *Main edging:* Join side seams. Starting at top of left front, with dark shade and No. 12 needles, cast on 13 sts. and work a strip in k. 1, p. 1 rib to fit down left front, all round lower edge and up right front; sew in position as you go along. Make 4 pairs of buttonholes in edging for right front, the first pair to come at top of front shaping with 10 rows between the 2 holes, the last pair ¼-inch from top of neck ribbing, and remaining 2 pairs spaced evenly. Mark position of buttons on left front with pins then work holes to correspond. To make a buttonhole:—Rib 5, cast off 3, rib to end and back, casting on 3 over those cast off.

Sleeves: Cast on 13 sts. and work a strip of rib for the bottom of each sleeve and sew in position.

TO MAKE UP

Join sleeve seams; insert sleeves. Sew on buttons to match buttonholes. Press seams.

36

Long Waisted
Counter-change cables give a firm all-over fabric

MATERIALS: Of Patons Beehive Fingering, 3-ply ("Patonised" shrink-resist finish), 9 ozs. for short sleeves, 10 ozs. for long. A pair each No. 11 and No. 9 "Beehive" needles. Nine buttons. Cable needle and medium-sized crochet hook.

MEASUREMENTS: To fit 32–34-inch bust; length from top of shoulders, 21 inches; sleeve seam, 8 inches cuff turned down, or 18½ inches.

TENSION: 7½ stitches to an inch over cable pattern.

BACK
With No. 11 needles, cast on 114 sts. and work

● The picture on the right shows the cable-stitch at centre back.

in pattern:—1ST ROW (Wrong side facing): * k. 3, p. 6; repeat from * five times more, k. 6, ¶ p. 6, k. 3; repeat from ¶ to end. 2ND ROW: * p. 3, k. 6; repeat from * five times more, p. 6, ¶ k. 6, p. 3; repeat from ¶ to end. Repeat 1st and 2nd rows twice more, then 1st row again.

8TH ROW (Right side facing): * p. 3, slip next 3 on cable needle and place to front of work, knit next 3 sts., then knit stitches from cable needle (this will be referred to as front cable); repeat from * five times more, p. 6, ¶ slip next 3 sts. on spare needle and place to back of work, knit next 3 sts., then k. 3 from spare needle (this will be referred to as back cable), p. 3; repeat from ¶ to end.

9TH ROW: p. 3, k. 3, * p. 6, k. 3; repeat from * four times more, p. 12, ¶ k. 3, p. 6; repeat from ¶ four times more, k. 3, p. 3. 10TH ROW: k. 3, p. 3, * k. 6, p. 3; repeat from * four times more, k.12, ¶ p. 3, k. 6; repeat from ¶ four times more, p. 3, k. 3. Repeat 9th and 10th rows twice more, then 9th row again.

16TH ROW: k. 3, p. 3, * cable front, p. 3; repeat from * four times more, cable front, ¶ cable back, p. 3; repeat from ¶ five times more, k. 3. 17TH ROW: p. 6, * k. 3, p. 6; repeat from * to end. 18TH ROW: k. 6, * p. 3, k. 6; repeat from * to end. Repeat 17th and 18th rows twice more then 17th row again. 24TH ROW: * cable front, p. 3; repeat from * five times more, ¶ cable back, p. 3; repeat from ¶ five times more, cable back. These 24 rows form pattern. Repeat them once more.

Change to No. 9 needles and continue in pattern, increasing at each end of next and every following 6th row until there are ₁132 sts. (Keep increased stitches in stocking-stitch until you have 9 extra at each end, then take them into cable pattern.)

Work straight until side edge measures 13½ inches, then shape armholes by casting off 9 sts. at beginning of next 2 rows, then k. 2 tog. at each end of every alternate row until 108 remain.

Work straight until back measures 20½ inches, then shape shoulders by casting off 10 at beginning of next 6 rows. Cast off.

FRONTS
Left: With No. 11 needles, cast on 70 sts. Work first 10 sts. in k. 1, p. 1 rib and remaining 60 in cable pattern as for right half of back. 1ST ROW will read (wrong side facing): Rib

10, k. 6, * p. 6, k. 3; repeat from * to end. 9TH ROW WILL READ: Rib 10, p. 9, * k. 3, p. 6; repeat from * four times more, k. 3. p. 3. When 2 patterns are done, change to No. 9 needles and continue on pattern stitches only, leaving 10 rib stitches on a safety-pin to be worked up later; increase at side edge on next and every following 6th row until there are 69 sts. on needle. (Treat 9 extra stitches as for back.) Work straight until side edge measures 13½ inches.

With right side of work facing, shape armhole by casting off 9 sts. at beginning of next row, then k. 2 tog. at this edge on next 3 alternate rows. (57 sts.)

Work straight until front edge measures 19¼ inches, ending at neck edge. With wrong side facing, shape neck by casting off 10 sts. at beginning of next 2 alternate rows, 3 at beginning of following 2 alternate rows, then k. 2 tog. at neck edge on next row.

Work straight until front is same length as back, then shape shoulder by casting off 10 sts. at beginning of next 3 alternate rows, armhole edge.

Rejoin wool to rib stitches on safety-pin and continue in rib on No. 11 needles until strip is long enough to go up left front when slightly stretched. Sew to front edge.

Right: Work to correspond with left, working cables as for left half of back. 1ST ROW will read (wrong side facing): * k. 3, p. 6; repeat from * five times more, k. 6, rib 10. In 4th and 5th rows from bottom edge make the first button-hole:—With right side facing, rib 4, cast off 2, rib 4, pattern to end and back, casting on 2 over those cast off in previous row.

Mark position of buttons on left front with pins, seeing that there are an even number of rows between each, then work holes up front edge to correspond; there are 9 holes in all. Stitch border to front edge.

SLEEVES

Short: With No. 11 needles, cast on 96 sts. and work 2 inches k. 1, p. 1 rib, increasing to 114 on last row by working twice into every 5th stitch until 6 remain, rib 6.

Change to No. 9 needles and work pattern as for back until side edge measures 8 inches. Shape top by casting off 6 at beginning of next 2 rows, then k. 2 tog. each end of every row until 20 remain. Cast off.

Long: With No. 11 needles, cast on 60 sts. and work 3 inches k. 1, p. 1 rib. Change to No. 9 needles and pattern as for back, but you will repeat from * twice instead of five times on first 8 rows thus:—

Press pieces on wrong side under a damp cloth. Join side, shoulder and sleeve seams; insert sleeves. Sew on buttons.

Make slots for cord round neck edge thus:—With right side of work facing, join in wool, make 3 chain, then 1 double-treble into next stitch of knitting, * 1 chain, miss 1 st. on neck edge, 1 d.tr.; repeat from * to end; fasten off.

Cord: Cut sixteen strands of wool each 66 inches in length, twist tightly, then fold double so that strands will twist together. Thread cord through holes at neck. Make two pom-poms and sew to each end as in photograph.

1ST ROW (wrong side facing): * k. 3, p. 6; repeat from * twice more, k. 6, ¶ p. 6, k. 3; repeat from ¶ to end. 9TH ROW will read: p. 3, k. 3, * p. 6, k. 3; repeat from * once more, p. 12, ¶ k. 3, p. 6; repeat from ¶ once, k. 3, p. 3.

Continue in pattern, increasing at each end of 17th and every following 4th row until there are 114 sts. (Keep increased stitches in stocking-stitch until you have 9 more at each end, then take them into cable pattern.) Work straight until side edge measures 18½ inches, then shape top as for short sleeves.

Lightning Source UK Ltd.
Milton Keynes UK
UKHW010851310123
416239UK00001B/96